"SECRETS OF STRONG FAMILIES [is] a *must* book for families and scholars alike. It is a major work of great historical and practical importance."
—*Rabbi Earl A. Grollman, author of*
Talking About Divorce and Separation, Living, *and* Talking About Death

"No one in the world has studied strong families as extensively as have the writers of this book. Nothing in the world could make human life happier than to increase greatly the number of strong families...a great treasure."
—*David R. Mace, Ph.D.,*
Behavior Scientist and Family Specialist

"This book provides the secrets to having, building, and maintaining strong families."
—*Sanford N. McDonnell,*
National President,
Boy Scouts of America

SECRETS OF STRONG FAMILIES

NICK STINNETT AND JOHN DeFRAIN

BERKLEY BOOKS, NEW YORK

We would like to dedicate this book to the three thousand strong families who shared with us the secrets of their successful family relationships.

And it is with love and gratitude that we also dedicate this book to two very special families—our own: Nick, Sr., and Tula Stinnett; Nancy, David Walton, and Joseph Shane Stinnett; George and Mae Morrison; Orville and Harriet DeFrain; Nikki, Amie, Alyssa, and Erica DeFrain; Margaret and John Schulling.

Reprinted with permission of the *Journal of Psychosomatic Research*, Volume II, T. H. Holmes and R. H. Rahe, "The Social Readjustment Rating Scale." Copyright 1967, Pergamon Press, Ltd.

Excerpt from "A Reflection: Riders on Earth Together" by Archibald MacLeish, *The New York Times,* December 25, 1968. Copyright © 1968 by The New York Times Company. Reprinted by permission.

This Berkley book contains the complete text of the original hardcover edition.

SECRETS OF STRONG FAMILIES

A Berkley Book / published by arrangement with Little, Brown and Company

PRINTING HISTORY
Little, Brown edition published 1985
Berkley edition / November 1986

ISBN: 0-425-09485-5

A BERKLEY BOOK ® TM 757,375
Berkley Books are published by The Berkley Publishing Group,
200 Madison Avenue, New York, NY 10016.
The name "BERKLEY" and the "B" logo
are trademarks belonging to Berkley Publishing Corporation.

PRINTED IN THE UNITED STATES OF AMERICA

10   9   8   7   6   5   4   3   2

Acknowledgments

Ideas do not develop in a vacuum. Nor do books. This book grew in a warm and supportive environment, nurtured by literally scores of friends and loved ones. Dr. Carl Whitaker, a seasoned family therapist, noted that there are no individuals in the world; we are only fragments of families. We wish to acknowledge, then, the families of which we are a part. Without them our little fragments would be nothing.

The university environment can be a rich and exciting place, and we have been fortunate to find ourselves in two special "families": the Department of Human Development and the Family, College of Home Economics, University of Nebraska–Lincoln, and the Graduate School of Education and Psychology at Pepperdine University. In both growth is a goal and encouragement an abundant resource. Students are probably the best source of energy in a university setting; their enthusiasm and idealism serve as constant reminders that life is full of goodness and there are many important tasks to complete. And colleagues/friends make the way so much easier. It is a pleasure to work with such a fine group of people — Hazel Anthony, Lucy Beezley, Eileen Curry, Karen

Eskey, Hazel Hutchinson, Charlotte Jackson, Dee Jakub, Lee Kimmons, Pat Knaub, Violet Kalyan-Masih, Kay King, Paul Lee, Herb Lindgren, Leon Rottman, George Rowe, Lois Schwab, Gale Smith, Helen Sulek, Sally Van Zandt, Rosanne Williams, Ginger Woodward, and John Woodward, among many others. Also thanks to Jeff Keuss in Seattle for his fine suggestions.

Good research costs money, and for the past decade we have been generously supported by the Agricultural Research Division, Institute of Agriculture and Natural Resources, University of Nebraska–Lincoln, for studies of rural and urban families in crisis and family strengths. A sincere thank you to the Institute and to its fine administrators: Roy Arnold, Dale Vanderholm, and Irv Omtvedt.

Appreciation also is expressed to Dr. David Davenport, President of Pepperdine University; to Dr. William Phillips, Vice-President of Academic Affairs at Pepperdine University; to Dr. William Adrian, Executive Vice-President of Pepperdine University; and to Dr. Martin Massengale, Chancellor of the University of Nebraska–Lincoln, for their encouragement of individual faculty members in these two outstanding institutions. We gratefully acknowledge the personal touch of these fine administrators.

Nick Stinnett recently became Dean of the Graduate School of Education and Psychology at Pepperdine University in Los Angeles. It was most difficult for him to leave Nebraska, but the family strengths research will continue now both in the Midwest and on the West Coast. Officials at Pepperdine have been generous in their encouragement of the family strengths research and very supportive.

We particularly wish to thank Suzie Sybouts for her excellent typing of the manuscript and for her helpful suggestions. Finally, our deep appreciation to the editorial staff of Little, Brown and Company for helpful assistance and encouragement throughout the project: Genevieve Young ("the best surrogate agent an author could ever have"), Kathy Moore, Glea Humez, and many others who have been very kind.

We are most grateful to the 3,000 strong families who shared the details of their lives with us. They are wonderful folks who made us cry and laugh and feel good about humanity. We have changed names and details to protect their privacy.

Contents

SECRETS OF STRONG FAMILIES

I

A Search for
Strong Families

Over two thousand years ago the son of a Greek sculptor was born. He became one of the greatest philosophers in history, having not only great impact in his own time but also throughout the centuries to the present as well. This philosopher's name was Socrates, and the hallmark of his sojourn on earth was the search for truth. He continually raised the questions "What is the meaning of life?" and "What do we want in life?" These are unsettling questions, but we must ask them because they prod us to consider what is truly important in life.

Today these probing questions are still being asked. National polls such as the Gallup poll and Harris poll periodically ask thousands of people the question "What is most important in life?" What do you think the most common answer would be? Money? Health? Beauty? Fame? Power? No. In a recent Harris poll, 96 percent said *to have a good family life.* And in a similar Gallup poll, eight of every ten people said *family* was one of the most or the *most* important facet of their lives.[1]

You may ask why millions of Americans today report that one of their most important goals in life is to have a successful family life. No doubt, one reason is that we experience our most intimate relationships within the family, and these intimate relationships have great power to influence our happiness and total wellness as individuals. Perhaps something deep within us realizes the family is the foundation of civilization. Perhaps we instinctively know that when we come to the bottom line in life it's not money, career, fame, a fine house, land, or material possessions that are important — it is the people in our lives who love and care for us. People in our lives who are committed to us and on whom we can count for support and help are what really matter. Nowhere is the potential for the love, support, caring, and commitment for which we all yearn greater than in the family. That is part of the truth for which Socrates searched.

A VITAL CONNECTION

Throughout history the family has been vital to the well-being — the survival — of individuals and of nations. If you think that sounds like a grandiose, sweeping statement, consider for a moment the pattern that has been observed in the rise and fall of great societies such as those of ancient Egypt, Greece, and Rome. When these nations were at the peak of their power, glory, and prosperity, the family was highly valued and strong. In a similar manner, the quality of family life and the strength of the nation deteriorated simultaneously.

We are overwhelmed daily with evidence that the quality of family life is crucial to our happiness, emotional well-being, and our mental health. We know that poor relationships within the family are related to many of the problems in society. It is obviously to our benefit to do what we can to

4

strengthen family life. This should be a top priority to us as individuals and as a nation.

ARE THERE MANY STRONG FAMILIES?

Pick up a newspaper or a magazine and you'll likely find an article or two praising the family and subsequently bemoaning its demise. As a society, we have collectively concluded that the family is our cornerstone, the "glue" which holds our civilization together, and that the family is falling apart, signaling our inevitable decline as a nation.

Nick and John serve in the roles of teacher, researcher, and family counselor and thus approach the question about strong families from several directions. As researchers with a painful knowledge of the sad litany of statistics on family problems, we agree that "Yes, many families are in trouble today." Our own studies of divorce, violence, and death in families underline a tremendous need for help that literally millions of families have.

And, through counseling people in trouble on a regular basis, we are profoundly aware of how family troubles can be the root of despair, madness, and death. As professionals we have been in the middle of just about every kind of family woe imaginable: child and spouse abuse, incest, child custody battles, suicide, alcohol, and other drug abuse. We get a fairly steady diet of guns, knives, booze, hate, slit wrists, and misery.

Added together, we have thirty years of counseling experience, both formally and informally, with individuals and in institutional settings. And although neither of us counsels on a full-time basis (because of research, teaching, and administrative responsibilities at the University of Nebraska and at Pepperdine University), we feel like we have heard just about everything.

John recently was talking with a social worker who gave him the details about a seven-year-old boy who is the victim of emotional abuse. His mother has a history of bizarre behavior and wild mood swings. As a result he had been placed with his maternal grandparents. His mother's monthly visits are still frightening experiences for the child, and on one occasion he was wild with fear the night before a visit from his mother.

"He was so upset he ate his tennis shoe," the social worker said, and then went on, as if this were an everyday occurrence, to other business.

Suddenly John found himself blurting out, "Wait a minute! What about the tennis shoe? He ATE a tennis shoe? What does that do to your stomach?"

"Well," the social worker explained, "he didn't swallow it. He chewed on it like a puppy, and spat the pieces out in a little pile in the corner of the room."

Almost as an afterthought the social worker added, "It didn't help his self-esteem much, when the grandparents served him the tennis shoe covered with ketchup for dinner that night."

If a child eating his tennis shoe out of fear of his mother isn't enough to convince you, we mention the man who teaches his five-year-old how to roll marijuana joints for Dad, or the family with the alcoholic teenager who has attempted suicide three times, been in jail repeatedly, tried to blow up the family car, beaten up another young man, and stolen rings and cash, all in the last year, as evidence that our rose-colored glasses were stepped on and crushed a long time ago.

But the families we have known, worked with, and talked to have taught us that families can also bring out the best in humans. With our families we can be happy, joyful, and fulfilled. Across our nation and around the world are millions of these strong families. We don't hear or read about them often in the media; we hear considerably more about the problems and pathologies in family life. A major reason for the sparse media coverage of strong families is the paucity of research focusing on family strengths. It was with this in mind that we launched an adventure called the Family Strengths Research Project, which would span every region of the nation as well as many other countries around the globe.

The story we tell in this book, then, is not one of sorrow and despondency. It is not a message of gloom and doom, though there is much to be sorrowful about. It isn't another study of why families fail.

Instead, we choose to tell a different story, a story of strong families. Over the past decade, we have had the pleasure to have personal and professional contact with thousands of successful families. They are from all walks of life, all faiths, all colors, some rich and some not so rich. They come from every state in the nation and many foreign countries. The common denominator among them is that their families are strong, and that they are willing to share their secrets with us. They helped us learn not how families fail, but what makes families succeed.

WHAT IS A STRONG FAMILY?

Although we know something about disaster in the family, we shouldn't assume that we know something, automatically, about strong families. To function as a healthy family is more than being *without* problems; strong families have lots of problems just like everyone else.

Before John's grandmother, Effie DeFrain, died at age eighty-six, she lay in bed blind from cataracts, both legs amputated at the hip from complications of diabetes. Her middle-aged son, Orville, was noting the difficulties he was confronting in life at the time. She listened to him patiently. "Life," she responded without malice, "IS troubles."

Our strong families know about trouble. We could tell you about the Nebraska rancher and his family who have been forced to sell everything and start over because of financial losses. Or there's the Oklahoma family whose father is chronically ill; they have had to make major adjustments. Or the young couple in Mississippi who lost everything in a flood except each other and the cat.

So, strong families have troubled lives, also. To be a strong family is not to be without troubles. It is much, much more: it is the presence in the family of important guidelines for living and the ability as a family to surmount life's inevitable challenges when they arise.

Strong families are pleasant, positive places to live because members have learned some beneficial ways of treating each other. Family members can count on each other for support, love, and loyalty. They can talk to each other; they enjoy each other.

Members of strong families feel good about themselves as a family unit or team; they have a sense of belonging with each other — a sense of "we." At the same time no individual gets lost or smothered; each family member is encouraged to develop his or her potential.

Finally, strong families are able to survive the crises that come their way. They unite to meet challenges; they are effective problem solvers. They pull together to pull through.

Perhaps strong families can best be defined as places where we enter for comfort, development, and regeneration and places from which we go forth renewed and charged with power for positive living.

THE WORLDWIDE STUDY OF STRONG FAMILIES

We have conducted many different studies of strong families, and partly as a result of this research a National Center for Family Strengths has been established at the University of Nebraska.

Nick began research on strong families more than a decade ago when he was an associate professor of family relations and child development at Oklahoma State University.

8

The first step in finding strong families to study was to make some basic assumptions of what strong families would be like. Using his knowledge about family relations as a guide, Nick made three assumptions about strong families: they would have a high degree of marital happiness; they would have satisfying parent-child relationships; and family members would do a good job of meeting each other's needs. Of course, this does not mean that single-parent families or couples without children cannot be strong families. (We later studied strong single-parent families.)

Nick and a team of graduate-student researchers then contacted Home Extension agents in each of Oklahoma's counties and asked them to recommend a few families that seemed to fit the assumptions about strong families. In order to simplify the analysis of the information collected, Nick also asked that the marriage be the first marriage, that both spouses be present (so that the marital relationship could be examined), and that the family have at least one child living at home (so that parent-child relationships could be examined). Home Extension agents were a good resource for strong family referrals because of their background training in family life, their concern for improving the quality of life for families, and their extensive personal contact with families in the community. Using the guidelines mentioned earlier, they recommended families they felt could be described as "strong."

Questionnaires were mailed to the recommended families. Included in the questionnaire were questions asking the persons to rate their satisfaction with their marriage and their satisfaction with their relationships with their child or children. Persons who reported a high degree of marriage happiness and good parent-child relationships were included in the study. A few persons were eliminated because their rating of marital or parent-child relationships was not positive. That only a few families were not included indicates the accuracy of the Extension Agents in their recommendations.

A total of 130 families contributed information about their family life. The families were diverse in terms of socio-economic status, race, ethnic origin, religion, and education. They came from urban and rural areas.

The questionnaire (the Family Strengths Inventory) used in the study was long and garnered lots of raw data. In fact, there was too much information to deal with in one huge chunk, so some data were stored for later use. Then as time and interest allowed, data were retrieved. For example, David Tomlinson, a graduate student at Oklahoma State University, was interested in the power structure in strong families. He went to the stored data to see how strong family members answered questions (who makes major decisions in the family and how those are made) dealing with power structure. Other graduate students conducted similar investigations. Some sent another questionnaire to the families and some conducted interviews with the families in order to gather additional information.

Using information from the Family Strengths Inventory plus additional information from follow-up questionnaires and interviews, Nick and his graduate-student teams looked at demographic characteristics of strong families, communication in these strong families, how they spent their time, marital need satisfaction, life philosophies, personality characteristics of strong families, power structure, parent-child relationships, family commitment, relationship patterns, how they dealt with conflict, how they dealt with crisis, religious orientation, and vital-total marital relationships among strong families.

When Nick moved to Lincoln, Nebraska, in 1977 to become chairperson of the Department of Human Development and the Family at the University of Nebraska, the research was expanded nationwide. John, Greg Sanders, and Karen Strand joined the research group, and a slight change in procedure was made. Instead of having families recommended, we asked for volunteers. Newspapers in all sections of the United States were asked to cooperate by running a small news story. The story said, simply:

STRONG FAMILIES NEEDED
FOR NATIONAL RESEARCH

Lincoln, NE — Researchers at the University of Nebraska are seeking volunteers for a nation-wide study of strong families.

"If you live in a strong family, we'd like you to contact us by mail," Dr. Nick Stinnett, chairperson of the Department of Human Development and the Family noted. "We know a lot these days about what makes families fail, but we really need to know a lot more about what makes families succeed. Your help is urgently requested."

Four dozen newspapers in twenty-five states printed the news story.

A few days later letters from volunteers started to pour in. Dozens of letters came each day for several weeks. People from several hundred families responded to the news story. When the tiny story appeared in the Minneapolis *Star* we got sixty-seven letters from strong families in the Twin Cities area alone. A Vermont paper called for information to write a larger story on the study, and responses from New England arrived. Papers in Iowa, South Carolina, and Oregon did likewise.

We were overwhelmed. American families were not going down the tubes; they were simply waiting for someone to ask the question "What is right with families?" Many people wrote letters thanking us for doing research on the positive aspects of family life.

We sent them by return mail the Family Strengths Inventory with more than a hundred questions on how their family functioned. The questions covered many aspects of family life.

Besides heartfelt gratitude, we could offer our volunteer

families little. Certainly not money. We did send them a short summary of the results of the project. But the major benefit they derived was the satisfaction of contributing to the body of knowledge the scientific community has assembled on strong families. Once again we gathered enormous amounts of raw data from the completed questionnaires. As in the work in Oklahoma, follow-up questionnaires were sent to some families and interviews were conducted with others.

After the first national study of strong families that we have just described, we went on to complete several more national studies and a few international studies of strong families, obtaining a different sample of families with each study. We won't burden you with lots of details about sample selection and statistical analyses of data. (See Notes for more details.) In some studies we obtained our strong families by running a news story — as we had in that first national study. For others, we have used the method of randomly selecting families` for the purpose of comparing high-strength families with low-strength families. Research has also been completed comparing recently divorced families with families exhibiting a high degree of strength. In time, the Family Strengths Inventory was shortened.

Graduate-student researchers have worked with us to explore various facets of strength in families. For example, Dr. Jerry King, a former graduate student of ours and now an associate professor of sociology at Arkansas State University, found tremendous similarities between blacks and whites when he made an intensive study of black family strengths in the United States. Julie Elmen and Judy Fricke, under our supervision, made a national study of single parents (both male and female), focusing on family strengths and how they are developed. Robin Smith and David Tucker studied strengths and stresses of executive families. Significant contributions were also made by Russell Porter, who investigated the strengths of emigrant families from the Soviet Union.

It was probably inevitable that in time our interest in

families outside the United States was aroused. "Would strong families in other parts of the world be like our U.S. families?" was a logical question to ask. Cultural differences could exist that might make interesting variations. As a result, the research was expanded in collaboration with Constanza Casas, who now lives in Bogotá, Colombia, to include Central and South American families. Verna Weber just completed a study of strengths of black families in South Africa. Bettina Stoll, one of our graduate students from Stuttgart, has investigated family strengths in a sample of families from Germany, Austria, and Switzerland. (See Bibliography for a more complete listing of our studies.)

The Family Strengths Research Project at the University of Nebraska continues to grow. We feel that we have only begun to scratch the surface in the area of strong families. Many questions wait to be answered. So, as our research budget and time allow, we choose another dimension of family strengths to explore. A new sample of families is selected, questionnaires and/or interviews are developed, and another set of data are collected.

As we write this, more than three thousand families have formally contributed to this research by completing the Family Strengths Inventory. About 10 percent have been interviewed. Most have been from the United States, with about 20 percent being from other countries. The U.S. families are a diverse group: they are from all regions of the country, rural (30 percent) and urban (70 percent), from all economic levels, two-parent and single-parent families, black and white, from all educational levels, of many religious persuasions, and from the early twenties to the mid-sixties in age.

THE SIX MAJOR QUALITIES OF STRONG FAMILIES

With the help of thousands of good people, then, we have an excellent idea of what a strong family is and how it nurtures positive approaches to life together. One of the most amazing things about the research is that six qualities were mentioned time and time again in our contact with these families. Not every family mentioned all six qualities, of course, but the pattern became apparent very quickly.

We found these qualities in the original research in Oklahoma; we found these same characteristics in the nationwide study of strong families. And in spite of cultural, political, and language differences, the strong families we have investigated outside the United States are very similar. Strong families share six major qualities:

1. *Commitment.* Members of strong families are dedicated to promoting each other's welfare and happiness. They value the unity of the family.

2. *Appreciation.* Members of strong families show appreciation for each other a great deal.

3. *Communication.* Members of strong families have good communication skills and spend a lot of time talking with each other.

4. *Time.* Strong families spend time — quality time in large quantities — with each other.

5. *Spiritual Wellness.* Whether they go to formal religious services or not, strong family members have a sense of a greater good or power in life, and that belief gives them strength and purpose.

6. *Coping Ability.* Members of strong families are able to view stress or crises as an opportunity to grow.

There they are. Six qualities that strong families have in common. It's all pretty simple. So deceptively simple that it could be misleading, because understanding what we need to do to make our families work happily together is only the first small step. Achieving is a great leap that takes the rest of our lives together.

Several of our strong family members have talked about learning this lesson:

"I've told you that we talk things out. We do; I don't think there is anything we [her family] couldn't discuss together. But that didn't happen overnight or without some work on our part. I've read a good deal about good communication practices, for one thing. And we had to gradually learn how to make them work for us. My husband has curbed his temper and sarcasm and I have learned to speak out — the popular phrase now is 'to be assertive.' "

* *

"The really good things in our relationship — the love, trust, caring — have developed over time because we have tended them just like a good gardener tends the roses."

* *

"You know the stereotypical story of the couple who have the lavish wedding, expensive rings, and exotic honeymoon and then settle down. The work is over. She gets dumpy and nags; he gets sloppy and never again brings flowers. We were like that until one day when we examined our life together and found it lacked something. Then we decided that the wedding, rings, and honeymoon marked the beginning, *not* the end. *We* had to renew the marriage all along."

Strong families are made. Step by step. People in strong families have to work at it, constantly.

The effort, of course, is certainly worth it. For a strong family gives incomparable support, satisfaction, and meaning to our individual lives. It can be the difference between despair and joy.

A Possibility and an Invitation

If we could wave a magic wand and create a strong family environment for you, we would — happily. But we cannot. You, however, can have a strong, happy family. "No, my family has problems," some will protest. That situation can be remedied. Others will say, "I already have a good family life." Wonderful! It can be *better* and *stronger*. Even if you're only contemplating marriage, you can begin to insure that the marriage will thrive beyond your golden wedding anniversary.

Be assured these are not empty claims. Why are we so confident of that? Simply because many people have accomplished these results and many more are achieving these goals each day. Marriage and family enrichment groups are very successsful because they help people change their relationships for the better. We have used the family strengths principles as a basis for marriage and family enrichment seminars at the University of Nebraska and have observed the positive changes that take place in people's lives.

The family strengths principles have been discussed by us in numerous professional journals, popular magazine articles, newspapers, and books, in radio and television programs, and in talks and workshops throughout the nation. Over and over again people tell us use of the principles has improved their relationships. And that makes sense because these powerful principles are not our invention. They have been shared with us by the real experts — thousands of strong families.

We think this book will become a very special possession for you. It offers a guide for you to reach the happiness and strength you want in your family and in other interpersonal relationships.

The ancient Chinese philosopher Lao Tzu said, "A journey of a thousand miles must begin with a single step." We invite you — urge you — to begin your journey to a better family situation by taking the first step. Come learn the secrets of strong families.

2

Commitment

—————◆—◆◆—◆—————

A FOUNDATION FIRM

Occasionally we are asked to single out the *one* most important characteristic of strong families. Although we are reluc-
tant to pinpoint one characteristic because we believe all six
are of vital importance, one could be considered the foundation on which the other characteristics are built. Our strong
families talked about this characteristic often:

"My wife bought me an expensive wedding ring for our
first anniversary. This symbolized to me that she thought we
were going to be together for a long time."

* *

"We give each other the freedom and encouragement to
pursue individual goals. Yet either of us would cut out activities or goals that threaten our existence as a couple. She has
a wonderful job that she loves, but she wouldn't transfer to
another city if I couldn't go happily, and vice versa."

* *

"Divorce is not an option for us. We do fight; sometimes we don't sleep in the same bed. There's nothing wrong with sleeping apart. You find out how cold your bed can be without your partner."

* *

"My family is the one group of people who has always had faith in me. I know that they're interested in what happens to me and that I can take any troubles home for help."

* *

"My husband and I decided that family is very important to us. Our relationship and our relationship with our children will outlast jobs and cars and houses. We have a goal of making our family healthy and loving; we work at it."

Commitment is the word that sums up what all these family members are talking about. The dictionary describes commitment as a pledge or obligation. Our strong families add to our understanding of what commitment is.

Commitment means that the family comes first. They said this in many ways:

"My wife and kids are the most important part of my life."

* *

"I'm encouraging my husband to take the children and fly back east to visit his father at Thanksgiving. I know it's expensive and the fall is a busy work time for him, but Pop is eighty-three years old. I want the children to know their grandfather. That's what family is all about."

* *

"What we have as a family is a treasure."

* *

"We have participated in several marriage enrichment experiences. Our marriage is very important to us; naturally we are willing to spend some time and money on it."

EACH PART IS PRECIOUS

In addition to valuing the family as a unit, strong families do not lose sight of the value of each family member. As one Florida mother commented, "Each person forms a part of the family and each part is precious." Their commitment to each other helps everyone in the family feel worthwhile and secure in the relationship. An Illinois wife provides insight into this:

"About ten years ago, after a brief physical illness and a change of jobs, something happened to me — to my mind and my emotions. I guess I became mentally sick. I lost control of my life. I became so depressed that I could not function. It was a living hell. Needless to say, I was not enjoyable to be around.

"Probably no one will ever know all of the causes for that bad period in my life. But I can tell you my family didn't give up on me. My husband searched until he found an excellent team of physicians to treat my medical problems. With their help, he located a counselor for me. He had to do this for me because, as you know, a depressed person has no energy or initiative.

"My daughter rearranged her schedule in order to drive me to Springfield for my weekly counseling sessions. We live about forty miles away. She planned something special for our trips to the city — some shopping or a nice lunch or a museum. That always helped to boost my spirit.

"My sister came by the house two or three times a week. She'd say she came for coffee or to talk, but she'd manage to tidy up the kitchen, do some laundry, weed a flower bed, or vacuum while she was there.

"After a few weeks of the deepest depression, I began to feel a bit better. My complete recovery took nearly a year.

"I am eternally grateful to a few close friends and to my church for helping in my recovery. But most especially I am grateful to my family. As sick as I was, I was always aware of their support and patience."

Experiences like that of the Illinois woman, Rob and Mary (whose story follows), and other strong families teach us also that people in these families are dedicated to their families — as individuals and as a unit — not just in words but in investments of time and energy. Their commitment is active and obvious.

BAD TIMES DON'T DESTROY

To the strong families, commitment is steady and unwavering. They're real people living in the same world as everyone else, so they have difficulties and hard times. Problems and quarrels and troubles, however, don't destroy their commitment to each other.

The story of one of our strong families illustrates this. Mary and Rob have been married for twenty-eight years and have three children. Their middle child, Erin, now twenty-four, is mentally retarded. They have united as a family to help Erin to become all she can be and to help each other. Mary devoted countless hours to an intensive home therapy program when Erin was young. Older brother Kit and his wife invite Erin to vacation with them each year and plan special activities of interest to her. Younger sister Judy helped Erin find a job and worked with her until she could handle it alone. The entire family has been active in advocacy for mentally handicapped individuals. Mary speaks of their commitment to each other when she says, "We are a team; family is the heart and center of our thoughts. We pitch in to help because if one of us is in pain, we all hurt. We aren't going to let any problem defeat us."

LASTING POWER

The other facet of commitment that the strong families reveal is that commitment is for a long time. Over and over, they told us that they expected their family to endure. Here is a sample of their statements:

"We were reared to regard marriage as a 'til-death-do-us-part kind of arrangement. I can't say we'd *never* (never say never, you know) divorce, but we haven't considered it yet and we've been married twenty-six years."

* *

"My son is in his last year of high school and I'm facing the fact that my relationship with him is about to change quite a bit. He'll be out on his own, married, and with kids in a few years. I remind him that things may be different but I'll still be his mother. That will *not* change."

Commitment Includes Sexual Fidelity

The world's most prominent sex researchers, William Masters and Virginia Johnson, after years of comprehensive sex research, concluded that one of the most important factors contributing to satisfaction in a sexual relationship is the presence of commitment.[1] Our strong families have known this all along:

"My wife, Denise, is very attractive, has a great sense of humor, and likes to be around people. And while I'm a fairly handsome guy and attractive to other women, I'm sure there are times when other men look more interesting to Denise than I do. There's always someone more beautiful, stronger, smarter, wealthier. But that's OK because our sexual relationship isn't based on those things. And knowing that there are no others for either of us makes our sexual relationship better."

* *

"Being faithful to each other sexually is just a part of being honest with each other."

* *

"I know it seems like everybody is having affairs — if you can believe gossip — but we are old-fashioned and faithful. I can only imagine bad things from an affair: hurt, deceit, family break-up. Being true to each other reinforces our bond."

* *

"For us, sexual faithfulness is essential. There is a security, a special feeling of knowing you are the only one with whom your spouse chooses to have sex. I think most people — no matter how liberal they are — can't handle affairs. When one partner has an affair, it does bad things to the self-esteem of the other. It gives the message you are not special, you are replaceable. It also gives a crushing message, 'You are not satisfying me sexually.' No wonder affairs don't work out well."

* *

"I can give myself completely to my husband because we trust each other. I know he is for me, that he values me. I couldn't relax to enjoy an intimate relationship with someone unless I had that security."

* *

"We promised in our wedding vows to be faithful to each other. We take that seriously. We could go looking elsewhere for sex, but what good is a broken promise?"

IF THE PROMISE IS BROKEN

Commitment enhances the sexual relationship and, for our strong families, commitment includes sexual fidelity. The two — commitment and sexual fidelity — are so closely linked in most people's minds that an extramarital sexual affair is regarded as the ultimate threat to a marriage. No other enemy seems as large as the "other" man or woman.

Because an extramarital affair poses such a potent threat, we believe it is important to sidetrack briefly to consider the extent of extramarital sex, the dynamics involved, and, more important, how strong families deal with such issues.

It's difficult to say, for certain, how widespread extramarital sex is in this country. For obvious reasons the Census Bureau has not added a question about it on its ever-expanding questionnaire. A lot of research and heated debate have been poured into the question, and we think that the best guesstimate is that roughly half of all husbands stray at least once at some time during their married life. In years past, it was thought that about one-fourth of all wives have sex outside marriage at least once. This may be changing, though. Opportunities for women are opening in more than the job market; possibly one-third of young married women today will have an affair of some duration during their married life.[2]

To make things even more complicated, the dynamics of affairs are difficult to sort out. Affairs are all uniquely different. To explain, some married people become involved with a stranger; others with a friend — maybe even a spouse's best friend. Some will have only one affair; others are chronic philanderers. Extramarital liaisons differ in duration too, from one-night stands to long-term relationships. One wife we interviewed was aware of the complexities:

"I don't know what I'd do if Chuck had a fling with someone else. I guess it would depend on lots of things. If he got drunk at a convention and had a one-night romance it would be easier to accept than if I found out he's had a three-year affair with his secretary. Although both involve sex outside of marriage, they don't seem exactly the same."

THE END OR A BEGINNING?

More than a few strong families have dealt with extramarital sexual issues in the past. We wish to remind the reader that strong families are not purer than everyone else; they have problems — including infidelity. How they deal with those distinguishes them from other families. Overcoming this crisis in the marriage was an important step for some couples in their long process of becoming strong. We are certainly not advocating extramarital sex as a way of improving marriage. Nor have any of our strong families recommended anything except sexual exclusivity. On the other hand, an extramarital mistake need not end a marriage automatically. We have on occasion seen extraordinary couples use such an incident as a catalyst for growth in a marriage, as the story that follows illustrates.

The snow was falling on that cold January night in South Dakota. The 10 P.M. news had just begun on TV when she took the sleeping pills from the medicine cabinet. She hesitated only slightly before beginning to swallow them — first one, then three or four together — until the bottle was empty. She lay on the bed, arranged the covers, and welcomed the oblivion.

The events leading up to that sad evening are divulged by her husband:

"Several months prior to this, I had become involved in an affair with a woman at the office. It started with pleasant conversations, long hours working together. I seemed drawn to her; my sexual interest was aroused. I began to fantasize seducing her and pursued the relationship with that in mind. It quickly became clear that she was attracted to me and encouraged my attention. The courtship picked up steam; we found many reasons to be together and soon we were in bed. The sex was quite good and we met regularly.

"One interesting thing about this is that I never felt like I became involved with Sandy because of any deficit in my marriage. All along I would have told you that I very much loved my wife, Anne, and that our relationship — including sex — was great.

"I think for me the whole reason for getting involved in the affair was ego. It was so flattering to know that a woman found me attractive and wanted me. Sandy always made elaborate preparations for our 'dates' — special meals or wine, candles, soft music. And she always fussed over me to be sure I was comfortable and happy.

"Our affair lasted for several months and we thought we were very careful to keep it a secret. Actually, people at the office figured it out rather easily, and I didn't want Anne to find out so I had a talk with her. It turned out she also knew what was going on; she knows me better than anyone.

"I tried to console Anne by telling her that I loved her no less because of this affair. It wasn't bad for a man to love two women. I even reminded her of books that said an affair could be a good way to expand a network of loving relationships.

"She didn't subscribe to that nonsense, and I don't guess I truly did, but it was a good rationalization. I continued the affair and Anne's pain and disappointment grew. Our marriage did begin to suffer.

"One day I realized that things weren't like my fantasy. I hadn't wanted Anne so deeply hurt and our relationship destroyed. What I had with Sandy just didn't compensate.

"I spent a sleepless night in soul searching. The next day I met Sandy for dinner and told her it was over. It wasn't easy, for I would have liked to continue. But I also was relieved no longer to be divided. I had a good feeling that I had made the right decision.

"I came home, anxious to tell Anne that everything was straightened out. The sound of the TV was all that greeted me and the house felt strange. I found her in bed, the pill bottle nearby. 'Oh no! Oh no!' was all I could think. The paramedics arrived quickly and she was rushed to the hospital. The next three or four hours were a nightmare. Finally the doctor told me she would live.

"I was so relieved and thankful. We began immediately to rebuild. The first thing I did was arrange *not* to work with Sandy any longer. (She was transferred fairly soon, and that helped.) Secondly, I began to court Anne again. We met a couple times a week for lunch; I brought flowers and gifts. We had 'dates' on a regular basis.

"During those 'dates' we had an opportunity to talk, and we talked out a lot of the hurt and bad feelings. I affirmed many times to Anne that I loved and cared for her. Finally we completed our healing process by restating our marriage vows. We celebrated our wedding anniversary by inviting a few close friends to a beautiful little chapel where we resaid our vows. Our marriage has now grown closer and stronger than before."

In another case, the wife had an affair with a fellow artist. Her husband stated:

"My first reaction when I figured what was going on was to shoot him. Then I decided to fight for the marriage in other ways.

"I gave my self-esteem a needed pickup by joining a health spa/exercise club and by buying some sharp-looking clothes. I felt better about me and life in general as a result.

"I was careful to keep communication open between me and my wife. I made a point of doing little thoughtful things for her. I knew if our basically good relationship deteriorated, we'd have less chance of making it through.

"I had some really rough days; I won't lie to you about that. My sense of humor helped to pull me through — my favorite thought at times was, 'Don't get mad; get even.' Somehow that allowed me to dissipate lots of hostility in a laugh.

"After a while, the extracurricular romance ended. My wife told me about it — turned out they didn't get together sexually as often as I had thought. They did more quiet talks, handholding, secret kisses kind of stuff. She admits it was an infatuation and blames it on midlife-over-the-hill-at-thirty-five crazies.

"We worked to reestablish trust and faith between us.

She doesn't travel to art shows alone. She could; that's just her way of saying, 'See, I'm not fooling around. You (or one of the kids) are with me.' She and I went on a weekend marriage enrichment retreat sponsored by our church. We've planned more family outings.

"As time goes by, the hurt is going away. I may never forget about this, but the memory will dim. We can go on to a good life together."

Hi Ho, It's off to Work

While an extramarital sexual affair poses a powerful threat to family commitment, many families have found their commitment to each other eroded by a more subtle enemy. Work and the demands of work — time, attention, energy — infringe on family.

What do strong families do about the pressures of work on family life? Obviously they don't quit their jobs. One thing they do is to keep reminding themselves of what is truly and lastingly important. A businessman from one of the strong families tells about his experience:

"Flashes of insight take only an instant and I'm not sure what causes them. I'm thankful for one I had on an airplane one afternoon. I was off on my usual weekly travel. Business took me away from home three or four days a week.

"I'd left a teenager disappointed because I would miss her dance recital. My wife felt swamped. She'd described herself as a *de facto* single parent. I had a growing sense of alienation from my family; sometimes I missed chunks of their lives.

"Indignantly I thought, 'Yeah, but they don't mind the money I make. I have work to do. It's important!' Then the flash of insight came.

"What frontier was I crossing? I wasn't curing cancer or bringing world peace. My company markets drink mixer. Drink mixer! Granted we sell it all over Ohio and are moving into the Pittsburgh market, but how many gallons of mixer for my family?

"I didn't quit. I enjoy sales and it's a good job. I make good money. I did learn to say 'no' to some company demands. And I plan my travel to leave more time at home. Sometimes now I take my wife or daughter along.

"In a few years I'll retire and within a few months I'll be forgotten in the mixer market. I'll still be a husband and father. Those will go on until I die."

Sometimes it takes courage to affirm the valuable things in life, as one wife explains:

"We felt like we were on a merry-go-round: no time for anything but work, no money, continual juggling of schedules and dollars. It was scary, but I quit my job, and so we had more time. The surprise was that we had more money as well. Because I have time to cook, we don't eat out as often; I can feed us nutritiously at home for half of what it costs to eat out. I shop garage sales and the thrift stores for the kids' clothes and household stuff. We sold our second car, saving gas, maintenance, tags, and insurance. All in all, we ended up with about fifteen dollars more each week than before — and we feel sane. When the kids are older, I may work again. Right now I am content to help them grow up, to continue my folk dancing, and to make contributions in ways other than a salary."

Other families shared similar stories:

"I could have the boat I want if I were willing to take a second job on weekends. Only problem is, I'd have no time to go fishing, so I wouldn't need the boat!"

* *

"We could have more things — a fancy car, new furniture, bigger house — if I worked outside the home. But we value our time together. Besides, someone needs to be there as a center for our family. Right now that's my most important task."

A second approach that strong families take in managing the pressures of work is to balance work and home. Many are sharing responsibilities for childrearing and housework more equally. Sometimes the changes are not smooth, as one mother of two explained:

"When I grew up I was Daddy's girl. I was sweet to him and he took care of me.

"Then I married Bill, and it was comfortable for me to be sweet to him and he took care of me. He would come home from work and I would hang on his every word.

"And then the kids got older, and I got bored. So I went back to school, and loved it. And I got a job, and I loved it.

"And for a while, Bill hated it. I didn't have time to listen to him anymore. And the kids hated it. Teddy cried in school because I was gone a lot. And David acted out at home to get my attention.

"For the first time in our married life the word *divorce* came up and we were both scared.

"So, we have been talking. A lot. And things are changing, slowly, steadily. Bill is slowing down in his work; he sees it isn't all that important. He takes more time with the kids and with me. And I have learned from watching him make mistakes, so I am not going to be smothered by my career.

"And the boys help with the dishes, and cook, and vacuum. They gripe, but they are getting positive strokes for the added responsibility.

"And we can't go back to the old way. We have changed. Growth hurts. It always does. But it is good.

"I used to want an ideal marriage. Friction and change were bad, in my view. I thought patterns of living were carved in stone. Wrong-o! The only thing you can count on in life is change.

"Oh, I have seen it happen other ways, too. Lots of time.

Bill and I are going to make it. Divorce is out of the question. I have seen lots of other women leave their husbands to be free. And in many cases I don't blame them, for the men could not or would not change. But I don't have to do that. My husband can change, and he is doing it. And I am changing, too. But I am staying. My career is important, but what have I gained if I lose my family?"

For many of the strong families, commitment means a promise by both spouses to make the marriage and the family operate as it should. Both husbands and wives are willing to change and to lend a helping hand to the other. The support and aid they give to each other (and to their children) are visible manifestations of their commitment to each other and to the family. A few of their comments illustrate this:

"His business is seasonal so some periods are quite hectic for him. I try to help by mowing the lawn and doing some of the other things he normally does around the house."

* *

"He helps me with the kids and around the house without having to be asked."

* *

"We were not able to make it financially any longer on the farm. So we sold everything and moved to town. My wife is teaching school to support us while I go back to the university to train for another career."

LOOK! UP IN THE SKY. IT'S A BIRD. IT'S . . .

More likely to be Superwoman than Superman these days. Many of the women in our strong families have wrestled with combining career and family. About half of the mothers in the strong families that we studied are employed outside the home. (This approximates the national percentage of working mothers.) What are some of their secrets for survival?

"I learned I could not be everything to everyone. No Superwoman outfits for me! I had to decide what was important and let other things go. For example, I have reduced community activities. It would be unrealistic to try to do volunteer work on top of everything else."

* *

"I have always operated on the idea that there is a point of diminishing returns. By that I mean a point when more hours on the job don't yield that much. If I get tired of my job or work myself into a state of nervous exhaustion, I'm not much help to anyone. I don't put in overtime unless it can't be avoided because I need to leave work on time and go home to refresh myself and enjoy being with my family."

* *

"I think of myself as having ten energy units per day and budget their expenditure. Work would eat up nine and a half if I let it. Instead I plan five energy units for work, three for the children, two for me and John. During rush times I may have to adjust to eight for work, two at home. At least this way I can always save some for home."

* *

"It helps to have a supportive spouse and children who are responsible (about chores) and responsive to my needs."

* *

"When I got my first job, my first reaction was 'How can I work with three children?' I was concerned for their care, so I located a good babysitter and paid her twice the going rate. I wanted her to feel responsible for the children."

* *

"When I can afford it I hire someone to do the housework."

* *

"We use paper plates for snacks. The children have chores; we use a chart to keep track of who does what. Some things just don't get done. The living room has needed paint for two years, for example."

* *

"I've always been up-front with the children about my schedule. Sometimes I have to say, 'There will be no time today.' They remind me if I neglect them too much."

WHEN LIFE GETS HECTIC

One working mother we interviewed responded to our question "How do you cope with work, family, and all your other activities?" by laughing, "Not very well!" All of us feel that way at times. The press to do many things seems to be part of modern life. Besides work, there's recreation, community activities, PTA, church, Scouts, sports leagues, clubs, volunteer work, and on the list could go.

How do we cope with the busy pace of life and keep it from hurting our families? We can get an answer from our strong families.

They are like the rest of us. Their lives get hectic and fragmented, too. But they control the madness. Here is their secret:

"I spent three days last week crying about how crummy things had gotten. I felt like a rat on a treadmill — running like crazy and getting nowhere! So my husband and I had a long talk and we decided that I will work part-time instead of full-time. I'll still have the contact with adults and the stimulation of my job (plus some money) but the four hours extra each day at home will allow me to do some things I have not been able to do. I want to spend more time with our daughters while they are young."

* *

"Things can creep up on you. No one would take on so many involvements at once. But through the years I had joined a fraternal organization, volunteered to help with the soccer team (my son is on the team), began teaching a class at church, enrolled in a class to learn how to do my own income tax forms, and began swimming each day at the YMCA. This is all in addition to work, yard, and car care. It was too much; one week I had only one night at home. I decided that I could hire someone to do the income tax, attend every other fraternal meeting, and swim five days a week. If that doesn't help as much as I need, I'll let the soccer team win without me."

We heard numerous families describe a family priority-setting session. The details varied slightly. Some families convene more often. Some write down their lists; others do the exercise mentally. The general principle was like that described by a Nebraska mother:

"We have a family council about once a month to review our situation. We discuss who's doing what, any accomplishments, new goals, et cetera. An ongoing problem is that of too little time and too much to do. We've found the best way to reduce the stress is to evaluate our involvements and eliminate some. This usually isn't hard. And it's a good learning experience for the children deciding what satisfies them the most and what they want to focus attention on. Brian, for example, has decided that he likes soccer better than Scouts. Matt opted to try karate lessons this fall instead of flag football. We knew that doing both was out of the question.

"I have been taking evening classes at the community college, but decided to put those on hold this semester. We have some major remodeling projects planned that I will need to attend to.

"We always finish family council feeling less tense and harried than before."

When fragmentation is the issue, each family member signifies his or her individual commitment by cutting outside activities so that family takes precedence. Andy and Patricia provide another example of how strong families go on the offensive. They are a young couple, beset by pressures — job, mortgage, car payments, church work, in-laws, the whole kettle of fish. They were so strung out by extraneous matters that there was no time for love. There was time to fix the transmission, or for the church ice-cream social, but not for love.

They sat down with their calendars and planned for the next six months. Here are their rules: "One night meeting a week. No more! No more than forty hours on the job a week. No work can be brought home. One date per week at least four hours in length. Yes, a date! Just like in high school! Only fun. Also, one hour of genuine talking time per day. Not per week, like so many people do, but per day. At the end of six months, plan for the next six."

Just as too many outside involvements, a distorted view of work, or an extramarital affair may undermine commitment, other factors may help to cultivate commitment in families. Our strong families mentioned four of these.

SOMETIMES COMMITMENT MEANS SACRIFICE

Athletes forego dessert, cigarettes, coffee, and late nights to get into top physical condition. Musicians and artists discipline themselves to invest the necessary time to refine their skills. Something else has to be sacrificed in order for them to do this.

The strong families who mentioned cutting out activities, civic involvements, or work demands in order to enhance family life realize that it isn't enough to give family their leftover time. Leftovers don't produce successful musicians or athletes. Why expect them to produce a successful family?

We usually think about sacrifice as giving up something really important. However, this is often not the case. Sometimes we discover, as our strong families shared with us, that we don't even miss the things we abandon in order to make a larger investment in our families.

One man we interviewed in Denver, for example, had just quit his job for the sake of his family. A few months earlier, thinking it would be nice to make some money, he had left a long-time career in education to become an administrative assistant to a hotel financier.

It turned out to be a jet-set type of job: lots of money, lots of travel, lots of flash, lots of fast-moving action. "The boss told me that if I worked hard like this for five years I would be a millionaire.

"That may have been the case, but in a few months time I concluded that I'd more likely be divorced or dead. I didn't like what I was doing. The long hours were killing me, and I missed my family.

"The boss was perfectly happy seeing his wife and children between eight and ten P.M. three nights a week. He thought that was about right for any husband.

"I'll get back into education. I suppose a lot of people would think me stupid to give up money and power for my family. The way I look at it, I was giving up more before when I was sacrificing my family. I don't regret my decision a bit."

At the heart of sacrifice is the ability to put the best interests of someone else ahead of self — an unselfish attitude. Repeatedly, this unselfishness is apparent in the comments of our strong families:

"Sometimes sacrifices have to be made. One time I may give up something for the benefit of my wife or child. At other times they do the same for me. No one feels martyred by this; there's a give-and-take to it."

* *

"I was both amused and pleased by a conversation between my boys yesterday at the zoo. The zoo has taped informational messages at each exhibit that are activated by a special zoo key for children. The boys immediately put up a clamor to have a key. They enjoyed the tapes but as we headed for the exit to go home the question of who would keep the key arose. Each said, 'I want it.' Then Dan, the ten-year-old, said, 'You can keep it in your room.' And Chris, who's eight, responded, 'No, you keep it. We can share.' It was clear that although each boy wanted the key, neither wanted to hurt a brother. The desire to be nice to one another was greater than the urge to satisfy self."

ONE HUNDRED PERCENT

Another factor that nurtures commitment in the strong families is their twofold involvement: in each other's lives and in family. This involvement helps each person feel a sense of belonging. One young woman described this accurately:

"I grew up in a rotten family, so I think I know a little about them. And as nearly as I can describe it, a troubled family is like a sieve. People drain in; people drain out. If you drain out, it doesn't matter much to anyone.

"I'm in a happy family now. My husband and his folks are wonderful people. It wasn't easy to get into the family. Strong families are closed. Not unfriendly, no; but you can immediately feel the love and the caring for each other, and they aren't going to throw that away for any outsider who stumbles in. Of course, I know they won't let me go away easily either. I belong."

An Oklahoma man comments on this total involvement in each other's lives:

"I like to think of it as being one hundred percent for each other. And an incident from my childhood demonstrates that kind of commitment. I was four years old at the time and we lived on a farm in Alabama. The house was set on a hill several yards from a busy highway. One summer morning my mother told me she was going to walk down to

36

the mailbox, which was located just across the highway, to get the mail. She asked if I wanted to go. I was busy playing and told her no very emphatically. I watched her walk down the hill. As she approached the mailbox, I changed my mind about going. I began to run very fast. As I ran I yelled, 'I'm coming! I'm coming!' What flashed through her mind must have been terror as she turned to see me nearing the highway. For she also saw a car — to which I was oblivious — coming at high speed. She knew in that instant that I wouldn't stop and the car wouldn't stop and I would surely be killed. She dropped the mail, raced across the path of the speeding car and scooped me up. We both fell on the shoulder of the highway. The car — which never slowed — barely missed us. My mother had narrowly escaped death saving my life.

"I've often thought about this incident in years since. It was one of my favorite stories as a child; I loved to hear it told and retold. Later we'd joke about Mom moving so fast. But as you might guess, even in times when I strongly disagree with my mother or become irritated by something she does, I never doubt her hundred percent commitment to me."

GOALS

The involvement of strong family members in each other's lives is also reflected in the number of goals they share. Common goals encourage commitment by giving direction and purpose to the family. Sometimes family strength is a goal; other times the family pursues an aim together as several strong families indicate:

"A good, happy, successful — whatever you want to call it — family is important to us. Whenever we get sidetracked from that, we remind ourselves and get back on track."

* *

"Our goals as a family include working this ranch and having fun together when the work is finished."

* *

"We pull together on many projects. Right now we're training our new puppy and doing some renovation of the backyard."

WE ALWAYS

Traditions in families have been described as the *we always* of family life: *We always* have cider at Halloween; *We always* have hugs at bedtime; *We always*. . . Our strong families often told us about their family traditions.

"We wanted our children to have a sense of who and where they are in history. We have continued traditions from my family and my wife's family. Oyster stew and carols on Christmas Eve are something we do and the kids know that Grandma and Grandpa did it when they were young. That has to give a feeling of continuity."

* *

"I traced our family tree several years ago and am glad I did, but the list of names and dates wasn't very exciting to the kids. We bought a tape recorder and have asked older family members — grandparents, aunts and uncles — to record what they remember: places they lived, occupations, how they celebrated holidays. We have also begun visiting areas where the family lived. We had good luck finding farms and old homes of grandparents and even great-grand-parents. Of course, farther back we only have county or city names. We have used vacation time to visit some of those 'home counties,' poke around in courthouse records and ce-meteries for traces of the family."

* *

"Each night when I put the baby down in his crib I have a ritual I say — even when he's asleep. It goes, 'Mama loves you. Daddy loves you. Your brother loves you. Grandmother loves you. You're a sweet, wonderful boy and we're very glad you're with us.' "

A Rose by Any Other Name

You may have noticed in the list of the six qualities of strong families that *love* is missing. That's because we tend to think of love as a feeling — butterflies in the tummy, tingles in your toes, fireworks when you kiss. And it is great when your spouse's presence makes you feel all aglow. But real life has moments when you disagree and days when the kids drive you crazy. Moods fluctuate; feelings change.

We prefer, then, to use the word *commitment* to describe a special kind of love — a love steady and sure that isn't subject to mood swings or the passage of years or hard times. It is a love that is conscious and unconditional. Commitment love says, "I decide and promise to love you because of who you are — not what you do or how I feel."

In the gardens of Arbor Lodge, home of J. Sterling Morton, father of Arbor Day, is a monument with the poem that follows. It sums up commitment love quite nicely.

> *Time flies.*
> *Flowers die.*
> *New days.*
> *New ways.*
> *Love stays.*

Putting It to Work

1. Have a family council periodically, say every six months. Ask family members, "How are we doing as a family? What needs to be changed? What are our goals as a family?"

2. Some couples have discovered a heightened sense of commitment by renewing their marriage vows. A wedding

anniversary is a good time to do this. Choose a special location — a chapel or a garden, for example. Invite a few friends to witness the event and have an informal reception afterward. Wear your wedding dress or veil if you still have it (and fit into it!).

3. Is your family too busy? If everyone in the family gives up one activity, the family can gain much more time together. Or rearrange schedules so that Mom has her meeting on Monday night while Junior is at soccer practice and Dad is out of town. Then everyone can be together Tuesday. Try to avoid Mom's being out on Monday, Dad on Tuesday, and Junior on Wednesday, et cetera.

4. Examine your marriage relationship for danger signs that may warn of an affair. We don't mean lipstick smears or blond hair; we mean signs that are visible before an affair begins. Dr. Carlfred Broderick, one of America's leading marriage counselors, calls these the three R's of infidelity: resentment, rationalization, and rendezvous.

Resentment involves any of the bad feelings or unresolved issues in a marriage that strain the relationship and make spouses vulnerable to temptation.

Rationalization is a process that most persons in adulterous situations go through. "She needs my help; we need time alone to discuss things." "He is misunderstood by his wife; I understand him so clearly. I only want to hold him and comfort him."

Rendezvous describes those opportunities that make an affair much more likely — candlelight dinners, traveling together to conventions, long hours working together.

Couples who are serious about guarding against infidelity can be sure to keep resentment cleared away. They can learn to recognize rationalization for what it is, and they can avoid rendezvous opportunities.

5. Read Alex Haley's *Roots,* James Michener's *Hawaii,* or Pearl Buck's *The Good Earth* together. Or read them separately and discuss them. These stories deal with commitment

in relationships and can serve as a stimulus to discuss commitment with your children. Laura Ingalls Wilder's *Little House on the Prairie* and other books are suitable for younger readers.

6. Rent a video disc player and choose a movie that deals with commitment in relationships or examples of good family life. *On Golden Pond, Fiddler on the Roof, Little House on the Prairie, Heidi,* and *Our Town* are some examples. Watch your selection together, have popcorn or cookies, and then talk about what you have seen. What did this family do that was good? How are we like them?

3

Appreciation

———◆·◆·◆———

"Last year I experienced one of my most bitter disappoint-
ments," says a New York woman who is a member of one of
the strong families in our research. "It was common knowledge I was one of the leading candidates for promotion to
district manager for the company where I work. There was
no question in my mind that I deserved the job; I wanted it
badly.

"I remember well the rainy morning when I was notified
in writing that I had not been selected for the position. I was
stunned at first. Later that morning someone told me who
had been selected for the position. The news was like salt on
a wound. The person who got the job was an adversary of
mine — a woman whom I disliked intensely.

"After a few hours, the shock and anger gave way to a
gray depression. I felt so empty and so much like a failure. I
called my husband at his office.

"As I began to tell him what had happened, I heard him

say to his boss who was in his office, 'Would you please excuse me and come back in a few minutes? I have an important phone call which I must take now.' The act in itself made me feel better. It was a kind of commitment and caring that he was showing for me.

"He listened to my whole sad story. I felt that all his attention was focused on me. And I can't begin to tell you how much that meant to me.

"When I had finished, he spent quite a while talking to me. He reminded me that I had done my best and no one can do more than that. So I had no reason to feel like a failure. He made it clear that the promotion wasn't going to make any difference to him and the kids in terms of how much they love and respect me. He reminded me that he loves me for who I am — not my job. He assured me that he and the kids are lucky to have such a wonderful person as me.

"The anger and resentment about missing the promotion didn't disappear instantly, but his expression of how he valued me helped me through a tough time. How lucky I am to have such a wonderful husband!"

William James, a pioneer in the field of psychology in the United States, once wrote a book on human needs. Some years after it was published he remarked that he had forgotten to include the most important need of all: the need to be appreciated.[1]

And, really, when we think about it, James is certainly correct. Why do we work so hard in our lives? Why do we beat our brains out to get braces on the kids' teeth? Or paint the front of the house? Or get a degree? Or a promotion?

Money, of course, is an important motivation. There's something deeper than that though because most of us have enough money to live. And in spite of that, we keep pushing ourselves. We really don't end up with ulcers purely because a Mercedes is all that rewarding, do we? And the pleasure of owning a Nikon camera or a mink coat or an Ethan Allen all-leather couch with real oak armrests can't be so great that we'd want to wear ourselves out, can it?

No. We could fill our houses with Mercedes and cameras and all-leather couches but these things couldn't pat us on the back and say, "Gee, honey, I really like that."

Appreciation is what we're really after so often. We want the kids to smile through straight front teeth that they love us for paying for all those wires and rubber bands. We want our spouses to recognize and be grateful for the hard hours we work to care for the kids and house and/or to provide income. We want to be valued for who we are and what we do.

As we scored questionnaires and interviewed the strong families, the quantity of appreciation they express to each other was startling to us. We had not anticipated this finding, but it leaped out at us.

The expression of appreciation permeates the relationships of strong families. They let each other know on a daily basis that each is appreciated. Here are a few examples of what they said:

"So often when we watch TV or a movie, my wife will say to me, 'I'm glad you are the way you are. You're good to me and the kids; you don't drink; you're not so wrapped up in work that nothing else matters.' "

* *

"He makes me feel good about me and about us as a couple. Very few days go by without him saying something like, 'You look really nice today' or 'The house is so clean and neat; it's a real pleasure to be home' or 'Great dinner' or 'I'd rather stay home with you; let's skip that party.' "

* *

"Each night before we sleep we tell each other, 'I love you.' Sometimes it isn't easy when we've had a spat or a bad day, but we still say it — and mean it. The spat will clear away; the love remains."

* *

"This sounds too simple, but Jane thanks me for everyday things that I do. If, for example, I wash the dishes, she thanks me. This helps me to know that I am not taken for granted."

* *

"I make a point of giving a sincere compliment to every person in my family every day."

* *

"He brings me flowers! Sometimes for no special reason."

So Very Basic to Family Strengths

"He knows I appreciate him," said a thirty-year-old wife. "It isn't necessary for me to tell him."

Oh, but it is! Very necessary. It is vital that appreciation be communicated. In expressing appreciation we, in essence, say to someone, "You are a person of worth and dignity. I am interested in you, and am aware of your positive qualities." That is a powerful message.

When we are appreciated by others, our self-worth is enhanced. As Dr. Don Clifton, a Lincoln, Nebraska, psychologist, puts it, we're getting our bucket (of self-esteem) filled. But our bucket is harder to fill than it is to empty. It's a precariously balanced bucket, and tips over easily, and can be emptied quickly by other people. "If somebody puts you down," Clifton says, "they've got their dipper in your bucket. By my estimate, it takes about ten positive strokes to repair the damage of one negative."

Many unhappy families have bucket and dipper problems. Spouses can't seem to say anything good about each other; parents criticize and belittle the children. Our strong families, however, have learned to *fill* those esteem buckets. A Kansas wife says, "He talks positively about me to others. Sometimes he tells me how people he works with will say bad things about their spouses. This makes him quite angry; he thinks it is terrible."

Another woman was especially pleased because, she said, "My daughter wrote me a letter after her baby was born and said, 'I hope I can be as good a mom as you are.' That really made my day! I'll never throw out that letter. I know I made mistakes as a mother. So does my daughter! How nice of her to remember the things I did right."

"Every Saturday my father goes to market," the daughter of a strong family in Germany told us, "and he always brings home some beautiful flowers for my mother. It is really a sweet thing for him to do and it makes my mother feel like a queen. The flowers have been a tradition since I was a child. Everyone in the family looks forward to them each week."

As parents we literally mold good or bad people out of our babies by telling them they are good or bad. We teach them self-esteem through our appreciation. The children in our strong families reflected this in their comments:

"My dad makes me feel real good by telling me I've done a great job when I make things out of Legos or my Erector set."

* *

"My big brother, Josh, and I were playing catch, and I was catching lots of times. Josh said, 'Wow! Wherever I throw the ball, David catches it.' That was last summer and I still like to think about it."

* *

"I like to read, and Mom and Dad always like it when I finish another book. Sometimes they give me a treat [for reading a book] like going out for pizza."

Pablo Casals shares some thoughts on what we teach children:

Each second we live in a new and unique moment of the universe, a moment that never was before and never will be again. And what do we teach our children in school? We teach them that two and two make four, and that Paris is the capital of France. Will we also teach them what they are?

We should say to each of them, "Do you know what you are? You are a marvel. You are unique. In all of the world there is no other child exactly like you. In the millions of years that have passed there has never been another child like you. And look at your body — what a wonder it is! Your legs, your arms, your cunning fingers, the way you move! You may become a Shakespeare, a Michelangelo, a Beethoven. You have the capacity for anything."[2]

THE RIPPLE EFFECT

From our strong families we have learned that appreciation helps family members to grow and flourish as self-esteem is boosted. As a pebble dropped in a pond causes ripples all around, so pebbles of appreciation cause ripples that carry into other facets of life. Listen to some of our strong families:

"Please don't get the wrong impression. Our family isn't storybook perfect, but we try to be optimistic. Money is short again this month but we say, 'We have enough to eat. We have plenty to entertain us at home: TV, music, books. We have much to be thankful about.' "

* *

"You asked what my spouse does that makes me feel good. Well, I'll tell you. She doesn't harp on my faults and shortcomings. Being a human, I have a few. She remembers my accomplishments, good deeds, and pluses. Sometimes I forget them and she reminds me I'm a pretty decent guy."

* *

"Our daughter takes violin lessons from a teacher who uses the Suzuki method. I have been influenced by the experience, too. Her teacher is rarely critical of how she plays. Instead she'll say, 'Your posture is nice today; now if you

47

move this finger more this direction, the notes will sound better.' I've tried applying the technique at home and it works there, too. Instead of 'Jessie, I asked you to tidy your room and you only did half of it,' I'll say, 'Jessie, the work you did on your room helped the way it looks. Now come back and finish it.' "

As you might guess from these examples, appreciation also helps to keep the atmosphere pleasant and positive. This is not surprising; we all prefer to be with people who make us feel good about ourselves.

We discovered another benefit of appreciation from our strong families: the folks in our research report healthy sex lives. We didn't ask them to count how many times they have intercourse each month, so we can't tell you anything about the quantities of sex they share. And we didn't ask what techniques they use. We didn't feel that either of these was truly important as an indicator of the vitality of their sexual relationships. The strong families confirmed our feeling:

"What do we enjoy doing as a couple? Talking and sex — not necessarily in that order!"

* *

"After all the years we've been married, she can still kiss me and make my heart skip a beat."

* *

"We bought one of those sex manuals once out of curiosity and a notion we might be missing something. What a hoot it was! Besides some information that I question, it was so mechanical. It made sex seem *very* difficult — not at all fun or even sexy."

* *

"Our sex life gets better every year that goes by. We may not make love as often as we did in the first years of marriage, but the intensity of feeling is much greater."

The quality of the sexual relationship is a reflection of the quality of the total relationship. Without goodwill, fostered by appreciation in all areas of family life, the atmosphere is not suitable for a healthy sex life. Sex simply does not begin at 10:30 on Saturday night with a shower and perfume. You've got to start early. Not even at 7:30 with a dinner by candlelight. We mean really early. Like Monday morning by taking out the garbage, and Tuesday afternoon by complimenting the children on their art work. Our strong families are aware of the importance of this total approach:

"The times when sex was best have been times when my wife and I felt especially close and in tune with each other — when we've solved a problem or when we're working on a project together."

* *

"I learned a long time ago that I can't gripe about my husband's sloppy ways, insinuate he doesn't bring home enough money, drool over Burt Reynolds on TV, and still expect him [my husband] to be very thrilled with me either."

DIRT AND DIAMONDS

Liberal amounts of appreciation do much to improve and strengthen family life. Many of us, however, have difficulties in either expressing or receiving appreciation. One reason we have problems expressing appreciation is that we haven't learned to be good miners. Let us explain.

South African diamond miners spend their working lives sifting through thousands of tons of rock and dirt looking for a few tiny diamonds. Too often we tend to do just the opposite. We sift through the diamonds, eagerly searching for dirt. Our strong families are diamond experts:

"My husband tends to forget birthdays and such, but there are other ways he shows he loves me. Last week, he saw kiefels (a kind of Croatian or Czech roll) in a Czech bakery and bought them for me because he knows how much I like them."

* *

"I ran my first marathon last week and finished fifteenth out of seventy-nine runners in my age group (fifteen to twenty years). I was disappointed at not being first and was thinking how fourteen guys came in ahead of me. Then Mom reminded me that sixty-four came in after me!"

Psychologists talk about self-fulfilling prophecies. This is a fancy description of the idea that you pretty much get what you're looking for in life. If you choose to follow a dismal path, you'll have your unhappy dreams fulfilled time and time again. And if you look for the good in people, you'll certainly find it.

"We fell into a trap early in our marriage — partly because of some other couples we saw socially. They considered themselves to be very sophisticated, and nothing or nobody quite measured up to their standards. One couple delighted in acid sarcasm — especially with each other.

"We didn't even realize how we were being affected until we left town that summer for a three-week vacation. We thought it was the trip that had made us feel better. We came back to town feeling good, went to a party at our friends' house, and came home in a depression.

"The next day we sat down to figure things out. We analyzed what was going on. The sarcasm, fault-finding, and belittling was rubbing off. We had begun to see things in a negative way. We were doing it in our marriage, too.

"We decided to stop. Our first step was to find some new couples to socialize with. We also worked on our attitudes. We chose to accent the positive.

"Now when my husband comes home he says, 'Wow! You've been busy with the boys today and you got your hair cut and did the marketing.' He doesn't even mention the weedy garden. And when he comes in disappointed over a sale he missed, I remind him of the three he made last week. We have conditioned ourselves to look at what we have, what we have completed, what we are rather than what we lack, what isn't done, and what we can't be."

Another reason people express appreciation so little is that they have low self-esteem. "Our daughter is having trouble right now with acne and other changes in growing up," shares a Nevada mother. "She feels ugly and clumsy. But to compensate she had begun cutting other girls (and boys) by talking about how bad Janie's skin is or how fat Elly is or how clumsy Bill is. We don't like her behaving this way, so we have talked with her about how she'll grow out of this phase. We have tried to get her to focus on her good points. I have bought ribbons and barrettes and fancy combs because her hair is gorgeous. We refuse to let her put others down and we balance her comments. For example, if she says that Elly is fat, we say, 'She'll grow up, too. In the meantime, she is an excellent student and musician.' "

When we don't feel good about ourselves, it is difficult to feel good about others. In dealing with people lacking esteem, it is important to be positive toward them. Teach them subtly how to show regard for others by showing appreciation for them. This is not an easy task, for they may be quite obnoxious; you might rather bite them in the neck and watch them bleed to death. Remember that people who have never felt the joy of being held in esteem are in no way capable of appreciating others.

We often are hesitant to show admiration for others because we think they may feel we are insincere or have ulterior motives. One California wife said it this way, "Now, if I told my husband that he was a great mechanic, he'd know I was lying. But he is a wonderful dad to our sons. He spends lots of time with them. They read and go to the park and go fishing. Not all dads are like that."

A father from New England said, "I hate to hear people

being phony in talking with children. I believe in praising mine, but I give them credit for some brains, too. I don't say, 'You jump higher than anyone' to my six-year-old. She knows better. I say, 'You can jump *so* high. You're doing good.'"

Members of strong families realize that it isn't necessary to be insincere in expressing appreciation, because each person has many good qualities and accomplishments. They all believe that if someone makes us feel good we should let them know. "I've encountered a few people who were skeptical at first. You can tell they're wondering what I'm after. I think, though, that my sincerity becomes apparent because I am careful not to use false flattery. If I don't mean it, I don't say it."

IT CAN'T BE MANDATED

Life might be simpler if we could pass a law that required the regular expression of appreciation within families. That, of course, is not possible. Members of strong families have discovered, however, that the expression of appreciation can be encouraged.

"During the first two years of our marriage, my husband was good about remembering our anniversary and my birthday. Then he sort of began to fade out. He forgot our third anniversary; I was quite upset and cried all night. He brought me long-stem roses the next day, but I felt like he'd only done it because I made a fuss.

"In the next several years he forgot several anniversaries and birthdays and we had a repeat of that third anniversary scene. I'd cry or be angry and he'd come in later with flowers or candy or a gift. At a friend's suggestion, I decided to try a different approach. Maybe, too, I grew to understand how busy and preoccupied he is with his work.

"Here's what I did. I began pointing out the approach of special events ahead of time. I do it casually and in good humor. I'll say something like 'That new Italian restaurant would be perfect to celebrate our anniversary next week.' Or 'Do you think your mom would watch the girls so we could do something special for my birthday?'

"I guess you could call those heavy hints. I will say that they've done the job. Jim hasn't missed a birthday or anniversary since I changed tactics.

"Some folks might not approve, I suppose. But it seems Jim needs the reminder. He's absentminded about other things so I know it isn't anything personal.

"We both feel better now. I don't feel forgotten or unloved and he doesn't end up in a no-win situation."

Members of our strong families mentioned other ways that the expression of appreciation can be encouraged. For one, they are good examples to each other and to their children.

Children Can Water the Flowers

The adolescent son of a strong family in Oregon said, "The habit of showing appreciation to other people I learned from my parents — mainly from their example of giving appreciation to each other and to me. They also helped me to develop this habit early in childhood by encouraging me to write thank-you notes and to tell others how much I enjoyed something they had done for me or given me. When I neglected to do this, my parents would remind me about it. This skill has meant a lot to me. It has made my relationships richer."

This Oregon youth was not unlike the other children in the strong families. One thing our strong families have taught us is that children can learn from an early age to express appreciation. They learn initially from very simple acts, but they build a foundation from which they begin to see the good qualities of others and feel comfortable about expressing their appreciation for those qualities.

As one father in Maryland said, "A lot of people don't bother to teach children to give appreciation, or even to say 'thank you.' They feel children are too young to learn such things. But they can learn. Children can learn to water the flowers at an early age."

A Colorado father told us, "My daughter and son periodically leave me notes. Sometimes they are taped on the refrigerator or bathroom door. Sometimes the notes are placed in my briefcase. The notes will sometimes just say, 'I love you.' Other times they will thank me for something nice I did for them. Yesterday they left me a note that said, 'We are sure glad you're our dad.' That made me feel about ten feet tall."

Yes, children can water flowers and fill buckets.

This Old Thing?

We've all had it happen to us. Someone does something you like or looks especially nice and you say, "Your speech was excellent" or "That suit is beautiful." And the recipient of your praise replies, "I thought it was too long" or "This old thing? I hate it." And there you stand feeling stupid.

Members of our strong families realize that the ability to receive appreciation gracefully is critical to keeping the appreciation flowing.

"My wife grew up in a family where complimenting was scarce. We had to adjust to that because whenever I'd praise her — on her cooking for example — she'd say, 'I know you like it, because you ate it.' I'd say 'Yes, but I like to tell you, anyway.' In time, she has learned how to accept praise and how to give it as well."

* *

"Our twins have hit that awkward preteen stage; they don't know how they want to behave. They eat it up when someone admires their clothes or tells them they've done a good job in ballet. And yet they're embarrassed. They don't want to appear to be puffed up, so they sometimes are silly and giggle or say the wrong thing. We're helping them learn some correct ways to accept a compliment. We have even practiced with them. They find that hilarious, but it has helped them to become more gracious."

Many of us are uncomfortable as the recipients of praise or compliments. We don't wish to appear immodest or don't care for the spotlight. Strong families, with their skills in appreciation, know that not accepting appreciation correctly can be interpreted as a putdown and stymies future overtures of appreciation. Several of them said something similar to what one Georgia woman remarked:

"I regard it as tacky to wipe out a compliment by saying something contrary to it. I have some responses I like to give when someone compliments me — depending on the circumstances, of course. I might say, 'Thank you for telling me (I did a good job or sang well or whatever)' or 'It's sweet of you to notice.' People like to be complimented in return."

A FINAL COMMENT

We often do an appreciation exercise in our marriage enrichment workshops. Invariably couples tell us that they do appreciate each other, and that they do tell each other. But we have them make lists of each other's good qualities, anyway. As the couples read the lists to each other in front of the group, the men often have big lumps in their throats, and the women's eyes often glisten. And as they finish and stand up to give another couple their spot in the limelight, they often protest: "Shucks, she knows all this stuff!"

But we know better. And even if she (he) does know it, it doesn't hurt to hear it once more. Being appreciated is like good music. We can listen to it over and over again.

PUTTING IT TO WORK

1. Write down ten things you like about your spouse. Five will do if you can't come up with ten. Be specific. Say, "I like the sparkle in your eyes" rather than "You're OK-looking." No mixed messages like "I like you even though you're sloppy." Don't put all your emphasis on accomplishments. Remember to appreciate people for what they *are* (patient, loving, fun to be with, gentle) as well as what they do. Share these with your spouse. The same technique can be used with children, parents, your in-laws, and other folks.

You can be creative in doing this exercise. One husband we know brought tears to his wife's eyes when he wrote all the things he loved about her in tiny letters on a small piece of stationary and put this document — more valuable than any mortgage or birth certificate — in a gold locket around her neck. A young woman had her father's positive characteristics inscribed on a photograph he loved.

2. Create a positive environment in your home. One way to do this is to begin rephrasing negative statements in positive ways. For example, you don't have to say to your child, "You fool, you spilled pop all over the table." You can say, "Whoops! Get a rag and we'll wipe it up." And you don't have to say to your husband, "Slow down, you pig! I'm not ready!" You can say, "I really like a good back rub and leg massage. That gets me in a warm and friendly mood."

We'll bet you can't come up with a negative statement that can't be phrased positively!

3. Try redefining the situation. This is a technique that involves mental gymnastics. Many faults that we see in ourselves and others are really positive qualities carried to an extreme. For example, the spouse who is stingy is really only a thrifty person in the extreme. Is your child loud and out of control or enthusiastic? Granted, the enthusiasm may need some curbing, and the tightwad may need to loosen his (her) grip on the dollar. The point is that we can view that person differently if we can see the core of good. Select two or three

traits of your spouse and children that annoy you or that are negative. Redefine them in positive terms. Here are a few more examples to get you started:

Spendthrift/wastes money	vs.	Generous
Talks too much/chatters	vs.	Likes to share
Domineering/bossy	vs.	Leadership
Always into things/messy	vs.	Curious
Won't follow rules/messy	vs.	Creative
Nitpicking	vs.	Attentive to detail
Meddlesome/interfering	vs.	Interested/concerned

4. Encourage appreciation by receiving it gracefully. It isn't necessary to say a lot in return to someone who compliments you. A simple "thank you" is sufficient many times, or you might say, "I appreciate your sharing that with me" or "You're very kind" or "What a nice thing to say." You won't appear haughty by doing so; you *will* make the person complimenting you feel good.

5. Develop your own special style of appreciating and remembering. We had a friend who kept lists of birthdays. You could count on him to phone about 6:30 A.M. on your birthday. He'd ask for the birthday celebrant, and when he or she answered, the strains of "Happy Birthday to You" on his trumpet would follow.

We know a woman who keeps her eyes and ears open for friends and family who are feeling blue or unloved. Then she sends a small gift or card signed "From someone who loves you." Invariably the recipient spends time trying to figure out who sent it and, in the course, realizes how many people love him or her.

6. Set a goal for yourself of giving one compliment per day to your spouse and kids. Some people find it helpful to use a chart to remind them and to keep track of their progress. Although a bit mechanical, the chart can be an aid in getting the new behavior established. As it becomes a habit to be more expressive with appreciation, you won't need the chart.

4

Communication

———•❖•———

How Many Out of 10,000?

We read about an experiment that boggles our minds. A researcher, interested in the amount of time that the average husband and wife spend in conversation each week, wired portable microphones to the subjects. Every word they spoke was recorded. Now maybe the microphone stymied some comments; they probably didn't yell at the kids as much. But guess how much time the average couple spends in conversation each week. Seventeen minutes. Seventeen minutes! By the way, there are 10,080 minutes in a week.[1]

The strong families in our research spend lots of time in conversation. They talk a lot about small, trivial topics as well as the profound, deep issues of life. One mother in Rhode Island makes a statement that is typical of our strong families: "We think it is very important to keep in touch with each other and to know where each one is. We want full contact with each other, not a lot of ten percent or twenty percent contacts!"

Good communication isn't something that just happens

among strong families; they make it happen, as the case of Andrea and Randy illustrates. Randal is an insurance salesman from Arkansas. He and Andrea have been married ten years and have one child. Their family is strong, but like all of our strong families they have encountered problems:

"Selling insurance involves a lot of traveling and a good bit of calling on people at night.

"If you don't watch it, your family can really get the shaft in this business. You can easily spend so much of your time working and traveling that your family never sees you.

"I slid into this pattern. I was out every night during the week, plus I was out of town on the weekends at least two weeks out of the month. I was with Andrea and the baby very little; I was becoming a stranger to them.

"One day Andrea and I were having lunch together and I told her I would be out of town again for the weekend.

"She exploded. When she calmed down she said to me in her no-nonsense manner, 'Randy, do you realize that you have been out every weeknight this entire month and with your going out of town this weekend there has been only *one* weekend this month you have been home? We have to do something.'

"She was right; things had to change. I started by canceling my weekend travel plans. It was more critical for me to be home.

"We talked a long time over the next ten days about alternatives. We made some key changes in our life-style and communication patterns. The changes have worked very well for us and have turned a bad situation into a good one.

"One thing I began to do was to telephone a lot when I traveled. You know, just so we could let each other know how we were doing and what was happening. It's a simple way that we can say, 'Hey, I care about you,' and we can stay in contact even though I am away. And the phone company loves it!

"We have a custom now that when I know I'm going to be getting home late I will let Andrea know and she will catch a nap in the afternoon. Then when I get home, even if it's after midnight, she will be up waiting for me and we can have a cup of coffee together. We often go for a walk afterwards. These times are very special for us. We look forward to them.

"Another important change we have made is that we now spend at least forty-five minutes each day genuinely conversing with each other. We periodically discuss our short- and long-term goals with each other just so we keep up with where each of us is at."

NO SURPRISE

"Each night when the children are ready for bed, we go into their bedrooms and give each a big hug and kiss. Then we say, 'You are really good kids and we love you very much.' We think it's important to leave that message with them at the end of the day."

* *

"One thing that means a lot to us is going to dinner alone [without the children]. We plan about three hours for this. We may have dinner one place and a special dessert at another or go window-shopping after. We get a lot of visiting done this way."

* *

"Whenever my husband travels he always calls home every day or so — sometimes every day. It just doesn't seem right not to talk with him each day. We get lonesome for conversation with each other."

While appreciation was the least anticipated characteristic of the strong families, the presence of good communication patterns was the finding that was the least surprising.

Countless research studies from very diverse fields led us to predict effective communication as a factor in building strong families. The strong families verified — in their own words — the formal findings about the importance of communication in relationships.

WHAT COMMUNICATION DOES

Although these are extreme cases, research tells us that people who suffer communication deprivation — such as in solitary confinement — often develop emotional problems, mental disturbances, or psychoses. In less extreme circumstances, people confined at home by health problems or old age often go deep into themselves. Our strong families commented on the value of communication to mental health:

"Our teenager came home from school very upset. Some girls had teased her because she hasn't begun to blossom physically yet. Fortunately she was able to talk to me about it. I could tell her that things were like that when I was a girl, too. Our chests are never the right size; girls get teased for too much and too little. She was able, after venting her hurt and anger, to say, 'Next time, I'll say . . .' She has several good retorts planned. We laughed about those. I'm so glad she didn't have to bear that alone."

* *

"I get overwhelmed at work; there's so much to be done *always* and not enough time. I come home and my wife hears me out and gently reminds me of reality again. She gives me perspective and hope."

* *

"Last week I had an ugly confrontation with a neighbor. My son and a friend had climbed her dogwood tree. She shooed them away and came over to read me the riot act. I felt like she accused me unjustly of being a bad mother and of encouraging the kids to climb her tree. I stewed and fumed until my husband came home. After I told him about it and we talked it through, my bad feelings began to go away. Telling it to him helped me release the anger."

Builds Belonging

No one wants to feel as though he or she is all alone in the world. All of us want to feel that we are a part of others; we need to relate to other people. Communication is the process through which we can relate to others as our strong families indicate:

"I found in my husband someone with whom I could share my thoughts, ambitions, dreams, and fears. I truly feel that we are two who have become one."

* *

"My parents always have time to listen to my problems or concerns. I know they'll have time for me no matter what. They're on my side."

One of the ways that communication helps us feel connected to other people is through the exchange of information. It's hard to feel close to someone you know little about. The exchange of information helps in another way, too.

Greases the Wheels

Repeatedly quotes from our strong families mention communication. Look back through the chapters you've read or glance ahead and you'll notice how often they say things like "We sat down and *talked* about it" or "We had a *long talk* and decided . . ." or "We have a family council (or meetings) to *discuss*. . . ."

Strong families face the same problems as everyone else: they overdraw at the bank, the car breaks down, the teenagers get acne, they get tired out, or you-name-it. The difference is the way they deal with problems. Good communication practices help to ease daily frustration levels by increasing the families' effectiveness in solving problems.

Because they freely exchange information and ideas, strong families are more successful in dealing with problems.

Do It Right

Marriage and family therapists pinpoint a lack of communication or bad communication as a major source of family unhappiness. We want to look at some of the things that strong families have learned about good practices. Their experiences help us to see how to eliminate faulty ways of communication in favor of effective ones.

The Grand Canyon Factor

A man stood silently with his son, daughter-in-law, and three grandchildren. He pondered the evolution of his family — his own marriage, the birth of his children, and now being a part of the growth and development of his grandchildren. His thoughts then turned to the sight before him — the Grand Canyon of the Colorado River in Arizona. He marveled at the incredible beauty of this national treasure. He thought of the millions of years that it took to form such a magnificent creation — all of it taking place without a sense of hurry or urgency. He whispered slowly and thoughtfully, "Things take time."

Things certainly do take time; good communication takes time. And this is a very important characteristic among strong families — they spend time in family communication.

As one father says:

"We spend a lot of time just talking to each other about all sorts of things. The conversations are usually not about anything profound. Much of what we talk about would be considered by many people to be trivial, but we just enjoy talking with each other, even if what we are talking about amounts to nothing.

"Funny thing is, sometimes we uncover important

63

issues — feelings or values that need to be discussed. And I've always felt that I couldn't expect a wife or child to bring the heavy matters to me if I wasn't interested in the less critical areas of their lives. If my son can't talk with me about cars and tennis, why should he think I'd listen about the drug traffic at school?"

Communication time is high on the priority list of strong families. While much of their communication is spontaneous — "We talk while we do chores together" or "We talk any time we're together" — some strong families plan a certain time each day for the entire family to be together to talk.

Oteka and Jerry, for example, use dinner as a time for each member of the family to share the most enjoyable experiences of the day. Other families plan special times, such as family night or family councils, for family members to share happy things, problems, and concerns with each other. At all times, the families do not shirk talking about difficult or troubling things; but at the same time, they make sure that positive sides of life are well represented in the dialogues. One father noted:

"If all we did was focus on problems I'd go nuts. People who dwell on disaster in their conversations make me wacky. I start drawing circles around my navel. Life is too interesting to be wasted by endless complaining."

Listen

An Indiana husband talks about his wife:

"Some people won't believe this because they think you have to be a fount of wisdom to help people and they don't see my wife, Dottie, in those terms. She is, though, the most important advisor I have. Not because she *tells* me anything but because she listens. She could teach classes on listening! She doesn't interrupt — except maybe to ask a question to clear up a point. She'll let me get it all out. So many people don't listen; they're just waiting for you to hush so they can go to talking.

"I find that I can take situations of all kinds to her and she'll hear them out. And the amazing thing is, without her offering any advice, I can see things clearer. Sometimes a solution will come to me as I talk.

"The way she listens lets me know she cares about me. She thinks what I have to say is important."

Strong family members realize that communication involves two steps: talking and listening. They avoid the trap of focusing on *talk* to the exclusion of *listen*. Sometimes they've learned the hard way, as one wife explains:

"When we first married my husband could talk more than anybody. He could go on for hours, it seemed. I'd wait for him to stop so I could say something, and he never would. I'd have to interrupt and say my piece fast to be heard at all. I began to be embarrassed by his monopolizing the conversation when we were with friends.

"And frankly, I needed him to respect me enough to listen to me once in a while. It took a while and some harping, but he saw my side and, with some work, he's learned not to monologue. We used a timer at home to take turns — kind of like you do with children. I'd set it for three minutes and he'd talk; then I'd get the next three — with no unnecessary interruption. As he learned to listen, we put the timer away. We also developed a secret signal — I'd adjust my left earring — for use in public to mean he needed to listen for a change. Once he was telling a good story and stopped abruptly in the middle. Then I realized I had reached up to brush my hair back and he had thought I'd sent a signal. We had a good laugh about that one later."

Listening strengthens the relationship between folks by conveying messages of caring and respect. Strong families increase their understanding of each other by being good, active listeners. One of our mothers describes what we mean by *active* listening:

"My eight-year-old began to complain often of head-aches at school. Three times in two weeks the school nurse called and he had come to her office with a headache and needing to come home. After a while I decided this wasn't a virus, so I questioned him about school. He just said every-thing was fine. His work has been good, so I figured he wasn't having academic problems. I pressed on to recess. I didn't get much, other than [that] Pat teased him over a missed soccer goal. I continued to ask questions over the next week or so and was careful to note facial expressions and voice tone as well as words. Several times it came out that Pat had teased, bullied, et cetera. He also had caused the class to lose library time because of his acting out. I began to suspect Pat was a 'headache' in more ways than one."

Active listeners notice facial expression, body posture, and voice tone as well as words. They nod or say "OK" or "go on" or something to indicate their attention. And really good listeners sift, as the nineteenth-century English novelist Dinah Maria Mulock Craik expressed it:

> Oh, the comfort, the inexpressible comfort of
> feeling safe with a person, having neither to weigh
> thoughts nor measure words, but pouring them all
> right out, just as they are, chaff and grain together;
> certain that a faithful hand will take and sift them,
> keep what is worth keeping, and then with the breath
> of kindness, blow the rest away.

Check It Out

Bob has been irritable all evening. He snapped at Ann a couple of times over nothing and has been silent for most of the time. Of course Ann is disturbed over this. Naturally she feels hurt and resentful toward Bob. However, such resent-ment is based upon the assumption that Bob's irritation and negative behavior are directed toward her. This may not be the case.

Ann checks it out and says, "Bob, you've been acting

angry and upset tonight. Is it because of something that I have done or is it something else? Do you feel OK?" Bob then shares with Ann that his budget has been cut at the office, and because of the budget cut he has to terminate a friend who works in his office. While he hates this, he has no choice and is very frustrated about it. If Ann had not clarified the meaning of his communication, she would have misinterpreted Bob's behavior.

An important technique of good communication that strong families use is checking the meaning of messages which are not clear. Unclear messages can often be clarified by comments such as "I'm not sure I know what you mean by that" or "This is my understanding of what you mean. . . . Is that correct?"

Vigilance in clarifying fuzzy or distorted messages helps strong families avoid two common communication pitfalls: indirect communication and mind rape.

A New Mexico husband tells of his experience with indirect communication:

"My wife's family uses a good deal of indirect messages and they understand each other. My family has always been pretty direct, so you can imagine the interesting misunderstandings Sue and I had until we figured this out. She'd say, 'Are there any good movies downtown?' and she'd mean 'I'd like to go to a movie.' I would answer the question she voiced by telling her what was playing. I might not suggest that we go to the show. Then I'd be surprised when she got angry or sulked. Eventually we figured this pattern out. She's better about saying 'I'd like to . . .' instead of hinting, and I'm better about checking to be sure I understand what she really means."

Mind rape is a term created by George Bach, family counselor and author of *The Intimate Enemy*,[2] to describe assuming you know what another is thinking without checking it out. James and Debbie talk about how they overcame this habit:

"We didn't know the technical term for it, but we were both a bit guilty of mind raping. I guess," admitted James, "the clearest example was over the issue of visiting my parents. ·

"I assumed Debbie didn't want to visit. She didn't have much chance to get to know them before we married. I'd fly out to Arizona to visit periodically. I didn't ask her to go; I didn't figure there was any need."

"Meanwhile," interrupts Debbie, "I jumped to the conclusion that Jim had some dark, ugly reason for not wanting me along. First I thought he was ashamed of me. Then I decided he must have an old girlfriend back home. I'd fret whenever he left but never asked why he didn't want me along."

James continued, "I stupidly assumed that her not asking about going was proof of her lack of interest. Finally my folks came here for my graduation. They enjoyed Debbie so much they said, 'You should come to visit with James.' That forced Debbie and me to face the problem and discover how dumb our assumptions had been."

Get inside the Other Person's World

We each live in our own unique world. No one sees life exactly the same way you do. The way you look at a certain situation depends upon past experiences you have had, the values in which you believe, and your personality characteristics. This means that when we disagree on an issue, it is not always because I'm right and you're wrong. It is more likely due to the fact that we come from different worlds; we have different perspectives.

People who are most adept in communication — such as our strong-family members — have the ability to get inside another person's world and to see things from that person's point of view. Social scientists call this empathy. Liz, one of our strong-family members from Tennessee, explains:

"Early in our marriage financial hardship forced us to move close to my in-laws. We didn't have to share a home, but we parked a mobile home on their farm. I soon learned a lot about my parents-in-law, but, more importantly, I learned a lot about my husband from them.

"Let me give you some for-instances. I had been disturbed by what I saw as Hank's habit of arguing — especially when I'd try to discuss something at meals. In my home, mealtime was a time for pleasant talk about ideas or events. But it seemed like Hank and I would always wind up in a disagreement. I began to suspect we weren't compatible. Then I observed — over a period of months — that he and his folks like lively conversations, and it isn't uncommon for one of them to play the devil's advocate just to keep things interesting. They don't get emotionally involved; no one gets angry or hurt. (That, by the way, is what clued me in that these weren't real arguments.) It's more like a debate.

"Another area of misunderstanding cleared up when I noted how Hank's mom keeps house. He and I had fought over housekeeping — I'd fuss that our place was messy; he'd say it was comfortable. When I got it cleaned to suit me, he felt it was too tidy, too sterile. One day it dawned on me that Hank's folks are more relaxed about housekeeping. They're clean — don't get me wrong — but they like to have books and magazines handy. She always has needlework materials out — on the table or scattered about the living room. And we do have taste differences in decorating. I prefer simple, uncluttered designs, neutral-colored walls, few decorations. Hank grew up with wallpaper designs, ornate furniture, and much more bric-à-brac. We've compromised on this one. And that compromise was made easier by understanding how each of us felt."

Create a Caring Communion

Rod, a pharmaceuticals salesman in Kansas, and his wife, Sally, a computer programmer, started their marriage with great expectations and happiness. Rod was just starting out in his business. His income was unpredictable, and getting established as a successful salesman demanded a great deal of time and energy — both physical and emotional.

"I would sometimes wake up at night," Rod said, "in a cold sweat because of feeling anxious about whether I would make it as a salesman. I worried about having enough money to make ends meet. Some months I made adequate income and some months I didn't.

"I was becoming an emotional wreck, but didn't share my feelings with Sally, I guess because I didn't think it was the macho thing to do. I wanted to appear strong and in control to her.

"But she wasn't fooled; she's very perceptive. One evening while we were walking in the park she said, 'Rod you're feeling pretty uptight about how things are going at work aren't you?'

"I told her I wasn't tense at all and that everything was OK. She didn't let me off the hook. 'Yes, you are worried,' she insisted, 'and I think it's natural. But I hate to see you feel that way. Let's talk about this and see if the situation is as bad as it seems and what action we can take to make things better.'

"At that point I opened up to her and shared all of my frustration and insecurity with her. I felt like a dam had been opened up inside me. I had not talked with anyone about this and it was a great relief finally to get it out.

"We talked about ways to cut our expenses and things we could do without and not miss too much. Then Sally asked me, 'What would be the worst thing that could possibly happen?' and I answered, 'The worst thing is that I would lose my job.' She then reminded me that if that happened we would still be able to make it on her income and that her job was very stable. We would have to make some changes, but we could make it.

"Well, that helped put things in perspective. The situation didn't seem nearly so bad. Then Sally said, 'I think you can be a great salesman — not just a good one, but a great salesman. I think one of the things holding you back has been your worry and anxiety. Why don't you stop worrying about work and start enjoying it?'

"Well I followed that advice and, you know, I began to relax and came to actually enjoy my work for the first time.

"My sales gradually increased, and today I am one of the top salesmen for the company. But that's not the most important part of the story. The most important part is that on that evening a few years ago, Sally was sensitive enough and interested in me enough to know that I was hurting and needed to talk. She cared enough to initiate the conversation. As a result of talking through that situation I felt closer to Sally than I ever had. I think that established our close bond with each other more than any other single event and it set the pattern for that type of caring, open communication."

We learn from our strong families such as Rod and Sally that communication in its highest sense is a communion of two people. It is a *caring* communion.

We mention in the chapter on commitment that strong-family members value each other, but they also let that valuing — that caring — that commitment — shine through. And at least two good things happen: they reinforce self-concepts and they set a climate for continued positive communication.

Keep the Monsters in Late-Night Movies

Remember when you were a kid and you would play the monster game with your friends? Someone would yell, "Here comes the green monster!" Everybody would scream and howl and run amok. The monster game was scary but fun.

Adults also play a "here comes the green monster" game, but the adult version isn't much fun. It creates anxiety, destroys good communication, and ruins relationships, because we do not want to be with people who play the monster game. We want to run away just as we did when we were children.

Strong families have learned to keep several communication monsters under lock and key: criticizing, evaluating, and acting superior. Their comments provide some insights:

"Mike never attacks me personally when we fight. I tend to drag up stuff from the past; however, I'm working to break that habit."

* *

"You know, parents can spend an awful lot of time fussing at their children, pointing out what they do wrong, and telling them they need to improve here or there. It can get to the point where children feel they are not pleasing their parents — that they're *bad* in some way."

* *

"I have an aunt who comes to visit about once a year. She's a dear woman and has many good qualities, but she always makes me feel like I am being measured. She isn't openly critical, but I can tell she's comparing my job, my housekeeping, my children, my life to what someone else has and does. I don't guess she realizes how much she threatens my esteem."

* *

"There's a couple that we've grown apart from. He and my husband work together and we used to socialize. Then she took a job outside the home and her husband finished a graduate degree and they moved into a new, fancy house. And suddenly I felt like she was looking down her nose at us. (He didn't change the way he acted.) She acted like she and I had nothing in common anymore. If I asked about the kids or anything like that, she would barely answer. She talked like she was too busy with work for anything else. So I asked about her job and she told me she couldn't explain; it was too complicated. I decided I wasn't smart enough or whatever for her anymore."

* *

"I'd like to brag about my wife just a little; she has such a wonderful attitude and manner. I haven't met very many people who are more intelligent than she; she's a physician — very respected in our community. It would be easy for her to feel just a notch or two above ordinary folks, but she doesn't. I'm sure there are people who wonder what it's like to live with her. I can tell you she never makes me feel defensive or inferior. I always feel she has genuine esteem for me."

Keep It Honest

The communication patterns in strong families are characterized by honesty and openness. People say what they mean and mean what they say. But the honesty is more than not lying; it is an absence of manipulation.

"It makes me angry to see a couple at a party in one of those situations where you know they disagree and he will argue his case and end by saying, 'Isn't that right, dear?' What can she say? That makes me very uncomfortable. Thank goodness my husband and I don't do that to each other!"

* *

"We became aware this summer of a bad habit our daughter had picked up. She was exaggerating her weaknesses (for lack of a better word) in order to get people to do things for her. I think it began when she broke her ankle and discovered how nice it was to be waited upon. Then we noticed she was 'no good at math,' so big brother was helping her by figuring her paper route bills. Or her ankle 'hurt too much' to help with chores. Or she 'had a headache' and couldn't go somewhere with us. We were able to correct her tactics by refusing to do things she could do herself."

* *

"My husband used to bully people in order to get his way. He would yell at salespeople, shout, or storm off with me. I knew early in our relationship that he wasn't truly mean; he barked a lot but didn't bite. After a while I tired of feeling pushed around. A counselor helped us identify and correct the problem."

Members of strong families don't resort to bullying, outwitting, blaming, dominating, or controlling. They don't play on dependency; they aren't silent, long-suffering martyrs to create guilt. All those methods of manipulating others lead to a falseness and shallowness in relationships.

Make It Kind

Some folks have used "brutal honesty" as an excuse to be exceedingly unkind. Our strong families maintain a balance of honesty and kindness. They aren't apt to let Sis go out in a dress and hairdo that look ridiculous because they don't want to offend her. On the other hand, they won't use one mistake in her judgment as an excuse to blast her taste, time management, hygiene, and study habits.

The comments of a Georgia husband illustrate the need to give kindness as well as take:

"I depend on my family for support and understanding. It is a tremendous comfort to be able to dump frustrations and anger on the sympathetic ears at home. I also realize that I can't just be the dumper all the time; sometimes I have to be the sympathetic ear."

An Ohio mother said:

"We practice our manners at home, too. 'Please' and 'thank you' are as important there as at school or work. If one of us is going to be late, we let the family know; it's just common courtesy. It would be stupid not to be as considerate and as pleasant to family as we are to strangers."

CONFLICT WITH CREATIVITY AND CARING

Without fail, whenever we talk about strong families, someone asks if they ever argue. Yes they do! And there are good reasons why. Jake, a retired tailor, with a good measure of wisdom puts it this way: "If you didn't give a damn about somebody, you wouldn't get mad!" Members of our strong families might paraphrase and say:

"When my kid doesn't do well in school, I get mad. I want her to be successful in life, because I love her so much."

* *

"When my husband drives too fast, I get mad. I don't want him killed."

Another reason for conflict in strong families has already been mentioned. They are real people in a real world. They disagree with each other; they make mistakes; they get fatigued and stressed; problems arise. Again, it is not the lack of conflict that sets them apart. It is the way they deal with conflict: they are creative and caring in conflict situations.

Current Events

One tactic that strong families use in disagreements is to air grievances while they are current. They don't hoard complaints to use as weapons. Jack and his wife are typical of the strong families in this respect. He says:

"We cannot stand to have contention between us. It bothers both of us to be at odds with each other. As a result we deal with sore spots as quickly as possible. Sometimes we have to wait a while — say until we get home from work or until we calm down a bit."

One Issue at a Time

A benefit of dealing with problems as they arise is that the families are more apt to be dealing with *one problem at a time.* Paula, from Virginia, provides some ideas as to why this is a good rule to follow:

"After several hair-curling arguments that started with the overextended budget and went to dirty socks stuffed under the bed to hair in the sink to both sets of in-laws to where to vacation, we wised up. How could anybody sort out all those things? If we could put socks, hair, in-laws, and vacations on hold, we could concentrate on the budget. We could handle *one* problem; that's manageable. Five problems at once are overwhelming."

Be Specific

"For a long time I was angry at my wife because I thought she was spending money too freely," says Tom. "I'd complain that she was spending too much. She'd say she couldn't cut corners any more than she was.

"Finally during one fight, she said, 'Just tell me how to spend less.' I began that she did a good job on groceries, she didn't splurge on gifts or things for herself, but she could spend a lot less on clothes for the children. Suddenly it hit me that that was my real gripe — she spent too much on the children's clothing. I said to her, 'I believe that is what really bothers me.' She suggested she *could* choose less expensive shops for the kids' clothes — maybe even use the second-hand store.

"It was rather funny. When I could narrow it down to my real gripe, she and I could deal with it."

Strong family members have a greater track record of successes in solving problems because a specific complaint is easier to treat. "You never talk to me" is harder to manage than "I wish we could have thirty minutes each evening without TV, the paper, or the kids."

Become Allies

Probably the approach of strong families that spares them the most grief in conflict situations is that of attacking the problem rather than each other.

"It would be silly to get caught up in personal attacks when we fight. All that does is hurt feelings and fan the fires. We try to see ourselves as being on the same side — as a team. The enemy is the problem. We're fighting it — not each other."

Ban the Bombs

A spouse or children can be devastated in innumerable ways. We think of these implements of destruction as atomic bombs. They're the weapons you hold onto for that last-ditch effort. Usually you're going down fast or are consumed by anger, and so you vent all your wrath.

Members of strong families have declared a freeze on such nuclear weapons. An Alabama wife tells us:

"I know more about my husband and children than anyone else does. I know their fears, their vulnerabilities. I have more power to hurt them more severely than anyone else does.

"So why don't I pull out all the stops and say those dreadful things that would wound so? Well, I feel like it might be winning the battle at too high a price. Generals make that mistake sometimes. My son is a World War II buff and I've heard him remark several times, '—— won this battle, but the casualties were terribly high. They won, but it cost too much.'

"I feel like it would be a serious violation of the trust we have in each other to use our knowledge, our closeness as weapons. Even when I get *very* angry I keep sight of that. To use sensitive areas as attack points is a good way to destroy a marriage or parent-child relationship."

Open Up Understanding

In conflict in particular, it is apparent that strong families put many of their communication skills to work. They check to be sure they understand what a spouse or child is saying; they actively listen to feelings as well as words.

One husband described a battle that failed to materialize because he and his wife checked out their understanding:

"I had been planning to send some money to my parents to help them through a tight spot. They're retired and had had some major expenses: Dad had surgery and a windstorm blew a tree onto the roof. Anyway I had the check ready to mail when Cindy objected.

"I could feel my temperature rising but asked, 'Why don't you want me to mail this?' She said, 'I want you to send it; I'm not objecting to that. I just want you to wait about three days so that a paycheck will be deposited to cover that check.'

"By controlling myself enough to be sure I understood what she said, we avoided a heated argument. If I'd jumped on her for interfering, being stingy, hating my folks, et cetera — well what a waste of energy!"

Part of developing understanding involves keying in on feelings. One woman we talked with came close to being profound when she said: "Feelings are real but they aren't always logical." She went on:

"For example, my daughter might complain that we're too strict on her. She feels confined and not trusted. When we look at the situation our rules aren't overly strict and we cannot find any evidence of not trusting her. She may admit as much herself. Yet it is clear she still *feels* confined.

"When we think together a bit more, it may become clear that she is anxious to be involved in several activities that require driving. She is impatient to grow up.

"Then I've discovered that the best thing to do is just to acknowledge her feelings. 'Yes, I understand that you feel restricted. This is why I think you do. . . . I'm sorry you feel this way; I believe it will pass. We might do this or that to help.' "

THE LIFEBLOOD

We want to end on a positive note because we do not want to leave the impression that our strong families argue all the time. They have their share of conflict, but they deal with it effectively. The conflicts become an opportunity for growth in strong families. Because they had good communication habits their disagreements are more like active problem-solving sessions than brawls.

And their good communication patterns do more than smooth the conflict; they sustain mental health and nurture intimacy. Effective communication insures that the commitment they have and the appreciation they feel are expressed. Communication truly is the lifeblood of strong relationships.

PUTTING IT TO WORK

1. Set aside some time (15–30 minutes) each day to talk with your spouse. Take a walk together or share a meal. Nick and Nancy like to get up early enough to have coffee and conversation before the boys are up.

2. Take as objective a look as possible at your communication habits. Are you guilty of monologue, mind rape, indirect messages? Most of us are to some extent. Pick one bad habit to correct. Focus on it for one month. Work on another next month.

3. Some families designate a mealtime as a time for sharing. Plan for the whole family to be together; share your most interesting events of the day at dinner or plans for the day at breakfast. Avoid disciplining the children or raising inflammatory issues at mealtime. Keep the mood pleasant.

4. Rituals and traditions are one way for family members to stay in contact with each other. Your family probably already has some traditions. Maybe you'd like to start some others. Following are a few ideas to get you started:

   a. Hugs for everyone at bedtime
   b. Games and popcorn on Saturday nights
   c. A canoe trip each June
   d. Egg hunts at Easter

e. Special stories at Christmas, Easter, Passover, Halloween, Valentine's Day, July 4, et cetera. Harry and Jody Heath have enjoyed reading *Miracle on 34th Street* for many Christmas seasons. They recommend it for anyone who no longer believes in Santa.

f. The Stinnetts celebrate Halloween by making jack-o'-lanterns and creating a haunted barn to thrill the neighborhood kids.

g. A barbecue and fireworks each July 4 or Labor Day

h. A weekend at a luxury motel each anniversary (leave the kids with Grandmother)

5. Marriage enrichment workshops are offered by a number of churches and other organizations. These offer a good opportunity to work on communication in the marriage relationship.

5

Time Together

———◆———

THAT MANY KIDS CAN'T BE WRONG

In a survey conducted several years ago, 1,500 schoolchildren were asked, "What do you think makes a happy family?" Children often surprise us with their wisdom. They didn't list money, cars, fine homes, or televisions. The answer they gave most frequently was *doing things together*.[1]

Members of our strong families would agree. We say this because we have asked many of them to do an exercise we call the journey of happy memories. We ask them to close their eyes and think back to their childhood. Spend five minutes or so wandering through the memories and then tell us about the happiest ones. And these are the kinds of things they come up with:

"I remember stories Mom and Dad told me when they tucked me into bed."

* *

"Going with Dad to work on the farm. I felt so important. So superior, 'cause my little brother wasn't big enough to go."

* *

"Having the whole family together at Christmas was special. All the grandpas and grandmas and aunts and uncles and thousands of kids. They made us kids eat in the kitchen together. I thought it was so neat then, and it must have been pandemonium."

* *

"Singing together, yes. Singing. We had an old piano, and I learned to play, and we would all sing corny old songs."

* *

"Vacation. We would go fifty miles to the lake and rent a cabin, and Dad would swim with us and dunk me."

* *

"My dad and I would cook together on Sunday. Lunch. It was great. We were all too busy during the week to take much time, but Sundays Dad and I would make something special like hamburgers or bean sandwiches."

* *

"Halloween. Mom would dress up like a witch, and we would decorate the basement and put on a scary 'wooo wooo wooo' record. All the neighbor kids would come down. Candy got so scared once — she was my best friend — she wet her pants. And she was eleven!"

Notice that the common thread in all these happy memories is doing things together. Again and again our strong families are characterized by the fact that they spend lots of time together.

THE NATURE OF THINGS

It is important early on to look at the nature of togetherness in strong families. Misunderstanding and misinterpretation are easy in a couple of areas.

Quality and More

A debate has raged in recent years over whether we need quality time or quantity of time with loved ones. Members of strong families have resolved the debate. A working mother of two children from Wisconsin says, "I'm a strong feminist and firmly believe women should not immerse themselves in family to the exclusion of everything else. But to excuse myself from spending time with my daughter by saying, 'It was only fifteen minutes but it was high quality,' is a copout, pure and plain."

An Arkansas man agrees. "My wife and I took one of those weekend marriage enrichment seminars. Two questions really hit us hard. The leader asked us to estimate how many minutes we spent in taking out the garbage each week. We didn't know what was coming so we answered very truthfully: 'About five minutes a day or thirty-five minutes a week.' Then she asked, 'How many minutes a day do you and your spouse spend in conversation?' You guessed it! The *garbage* got more time! We're fooling ourselves if we think that five minutes a day is enough time to maintain a marriage. And it certainly isn't enough to make the marriage grow."

George Rekers, a family therapist, uses a story about a steak to make clear the relationship between quality and quantity. He asks that you imagine you've gone to a new gourmet restaurant and that you decide to treat yourself to their best steak even though it costs $18.00. The steak arrives on an expensive china plate, served with flair by an impeccably dressed waiter. You note with shock and dismay that the steak is a one-inch cube. In horror, you question the waiter, who assures you that quality is what counts and this steak is *the best*. But if you're very hungry, you know that quantity also counts.[2]

Strong families realize that quantity and quality go hand in hand. The time they spend together needs to be good time; no one enjoys hours of bickering, arguing, pouting, or bullying. Time also needs to be sufficient; quality interaction isn't likely to develop in a few minutes together.

Abundant but Not Stifling

Our strong families work, play, attend church or synagogue, vacation together, and regularly eat meals together. Yet their togetherness is not smothering, for it has boundaries. Individuals are not swallowed up and lost in the group.

The balance between too much and not enough individualism is critical. Families are destroyed when they go to either of two extremes: If they allow the world and its cares and seductors to draw them apart, or if they for a number of reasons become so fixated on each other that they lose their individual identities in the process. Our strong families said this in other ways:

"My wife goes out every Wednesday to folk dance. This is *not* my cup of tea at all. So I enjoy the time with the kids and when my wife comes in at eleven P.M. she is full of enthusiasm and good stories. She is refreshed and Thursdays are better for it."

* *

"I have a very busy, very satisfying career at the university. The danger for me and my husband is not that I'll lose my identity (or he lose his), but that we'll grow apart. If I'm not careful, my life could fill up and squeeze him out. So we are sure to spend time together each day. We're especially fond of walks in the evening. Away from phones and interruptions, we share what has happened, make plans, and stay in touch."

A Minnesota mother mentions another important way the togetherness in strong families is kept from smothering the individuals:

"We do many things as a family but we don't always all of us do everything together. Being together may mean my daughter and me going shopping or my son and me going to his karate class or me and both kids at the library. My husband and I spend time without the kids; the kids do things together. It's a mix-up of twos or threes as often as it is all four of us together. Sooner or later we each spend time with everyone else in the family. And those one-on-one relationships — mother-daughter, father-daughter, mother-son, father-son, husband-wife, brother-sister — have a chance to develop too."

Planned but Not Mechanical

One of the realities of modern life is that many activities and persons compete for our attention and time. Almost everyone has a closet or drawer full of projects to finish — "someday when I have a little free time." Strong families are not exempted from the shortage of time but they have learned some valuable truths:

"We discovered fairly soon in our parenting years that family times don't just happen. They have to be planned. If we don't watch out, we end up scattered all over the town — Carl working at his office; me at bridge, League of Women Voters, or PTA; the kids at band practice, basketball, or a friend's house."

* *

"Our church — we're Mormons — encourages families to set aside one night each week as Family Night. No one may plan outside activities or have friends over to visit on that night. We have ours on Mondays. We do different things. In the summer we may cook out and play yard games. Sometimes we work on a project like setting up our aquarium. In winter we use the fireplace a lot — to pop popcorn or toast nuts — and to gather around to read mystery stories aloud.

"We try to do a variety of things so that Family Night doesn't get to be routine and dull. And of course, we spend other time together too. You can't just designate Monday as family time and let it go at that. That's like taking a bath only on Saturday night."

The story that one father shared with us was especially touching and impressive. It has to do with time together not having to be regimented and mechanical.

At age forty, this father had just about everything—professionally, that is. He was awarded a Ph.D. from Harvard at a very young age. He had become a full professor quickly, by writing books, books, and more books very quickly.

His life fell apart even more quickly. His wife packed her bags to leave him one Monday morning that spring. His best friend was buried on Tuesday morning ("He died from writing nine books and drinking to steady his hand when he picked up the phone to dicker with his publishers or creditors"). His brother had developed throat cancer from cigarettes, which he smoked to calm himself from overwork, and had his larynx removed on Friday morning.

"I looked at their lives, and I cried. And then I looked at my life, and I cried." And he began to change his life.

He scheduled in free time for himself and time for his family. At first he wondered, "What will we *do* in this time?" And then he remembered, "The history of science, the history of human exploration, is full of examples of experiments or quests that began for no particular reason and ended up with marvelous results. Think about it! Christopher Columbus was simply looking for a way to connect Europe with the spice merchants in the Orient. But he accidentally stumbled onto something infinitely more valuable than pepper. He ran into America."

He decided that chatting with his young sons while they had snacks or holding the baby as his wife slept might be the beginning of a wonderful quest. And because he had seen a new way to live, this story has a happy ending. His wife and he visited a family therapist and ironed out their difficulties, and the family is back on the right track.

Strong families seem to sense that much of what they do to preserve and enrich their lives together is done in their times together. So do they spend a lot of time "doing nothing"? No. More precisely, they are not worried about being with each other with no particular goal in mind. They know that in the long view, good things happen as a result of shared times.

PROFILE OF AN ASSASSIN

A recent newspaper story outlined historical researchers' studies of the lives and backgrounds of numerous modern assassins. The investigators concluded that the assassins shared a number of characteristics, including isolation, loneliness, and a feeling of being apart from the rest of the world.

We mention this because it underscores one of the benefits of shared family time: an antidote to isolation, loneliness, and alienation. Our strong families would agree. A mother from Maine noted:

"We spend time together because we like each other. It isn't like this-is-a-good-thing-to-do-so-we'd-better-plan-time-together. We enjoy each other's company. Frankly, I get lonesome for my husband and kids when we're apart for very long."

A New York father said:

"I had a disturbing experience when I was forty-three years old. I lost a battle with a hepatitis bug and was confined at home for several months to recuperate. My colleagues at work called to inquire about me at first and then drifted away. Except for two close friends and my family, everyone else forgot about my difficulties in a hurry. I don't blame them, and I'm not bitter or complaining. I've been guilty myself. What the experience did was make me realize which people truly are important to me. I'm really fortunate to have a wife and daughters, a mother (my father is dead), a brother, in-laws, and a few close friends who care. Spending time with these folks isn't a luxury; it's a necessity. They save me from being lost and alone."

A FAMILY IDENTITY

A second benefit of spending time together is that the family develops an identity — a group unity and a sense of their place in history. Strong family members talked about family identity in these ways. An Oklahoma woman said:

"I remember visiting my Ohio grandmother, aunts, uncles, and cousins each summer. Without fail, the adults would comment on how much my sister and I had grown and would add, 'They sure have the Johnson eyes and hair.' Dark brown — almost black — eye color and dark brown hair do run in the family. Hearing that summer after summer reinforced the feeling that I was connected to these people even though I only saw them once a year."

A Nebraska man commented:

"When the children were younger we always read to them at bedtime. Now we go to their rooms for a quiet talk before they sleep. Sometimes my wife and I go together; sometimes just one of us goes. We sit on the bed and talk about pleasant events or plans, usually for ten minutes or so. It's a special, private time with each child that makes us feel much closer."

An Ohio man mentioned:

"Photographs are very important to us. We have albums and albums full plus a huge box of them that need to be put into albums. All the important events in our family have been recorded — our wedding, the births and growth of the children, vacations, first days of school, new cars and houses, pets, and on it goes. The kids love to look at the pictures and see what they looked like as babies; our seventeen-year-old looks remarkably like her mother's wedding photo — when she was twenty.

"In this part of the country, tornadoes occasionally wipe houses completely out. I've thought that if that ever happened to us, the material thing I would miss the most would be our family photographs."

NOT A BANG BUT A WHIMPER

Hostility and violence are elements in about one-third of the divorces each year in this country. And certainly many unhappy families are plagued with anger and strong emotions. But many therapists feel that most family dissatisfaction and dissolution revolve around a lack of emotion. The spouses don't hate each other; they feel no anger. They don't truly love or care, either. The relationships simply fizzle and die.

Over and over our strong families have told us that relationships must be nurtured — like a plant or a baby. Otherwise they fail to grow. In their time together strong families nurture relationships. Their comments increase our understanding:

"We spend as much time working together as playing. There are always dishes to wash, laundry to fold, grass to mow, leaves to rake. But that isn't bad by any means. We have had some of our best, closest times working together."

* *

"We've just spent a couple of weeks at my folks' home, and one of the joys of the visit has been watching our toddler and his grandparents together. Granddad has read bunches of books to him. Danny brings them and dumps the books in Granddad's lap and crawls up. Naturally Dad drops whatever else to read to him.

"Danny and Grandma go out for special walks. They hunt lizards or crickets or rolypoly bugs; they smell flowers and watch birds; they wade in the puddles left by the rain.

Grandma has a cache of M & M's that she and Danny keep as their secret.

"I'd be pressed to say who has the most fun. I am thankful for the time they're having together. Mom and Dad are thoroughly enjoying it and Danny's life is definitely enriched."

* *

"My husband and I like to sneak away about twice a year just by ourselves. Chicago is a favorite place to go for our escape weekends. It's close enough that we can drive there in a couple of hours and there's always something — museum exhibit, theater, or show — to do. We need those times to concentrate on each other. We dress up and put on our best manners; we flirt with each other. Maybe that sounds silly, but it makes us feel more like we did when we were dating. In a sexy dress and perfume, holding hands over a French dinner by candlelight, I feel different than in jeans at McDonald's wrestling the kids."

JUST EXACTLY WHAT?

Families benefit from shared time because it eases loneliness and isolation, nurtures relationships, and creates a family identity. Fine. Exactly what do strong families do when they're together? Just about anything and everything.

Meals

Many, many times families mentioned that they eat meals together on a regular basis. One Idaho mother told us:

"We eat the evening meal together. In extreme cases, one of us may not be there, but everyone knows that being absent from dinner is not taken lightly. We use that time to share triumphs and tribulations. In a hectic world we need some common ground where we can meet."

Another mother in North Carolina added:

"We always eat dinner together and try to be together for breakfast as well. And we have a rule of no television during meals."

House and Yard Chores

"I grew up on a farm so maybe my background differs from some of the people you've talked with," began one Nebraska man. "But a lot of the time I shared with my parents was working time. I helped feed the animals, gathered eggs, weeded the garden, picked produce out of the garden, and generally helped around the house. It wasn't like I had a list of chores and worked alone. Dad and I would do the feeding; Mom and I would pick and prepare vegetables. We'd sweat and complain, laugh and talk as we worked."

Strong families have learned to make the time necessary for running a household into an opportunity to get together and to communicate. Some of their comments illustrate:

"I work until late in the afternoon, so I need help getting dinner ready. At first my son protested having to cook, but I've convinced him that there may be many times when knowing how to cook will be handy. Now he's proud of his accomplishments. He often has cookies or a cake ready before I get home.

"My daughter is still a little young to handle very hot things or knives, but she sets the table and likes to make simple tossed salads or fruit salads.

"We all get in the kitchen and talk about what went on at school and work while we fix dinner. They're learning other valuable things besides cooking; they're learning they are important in making our family run. That increases confidence and esteem."

* *

"When I find myself tempted to shoo the kids so I can get a job done faster without their 'help,' I remind myself that helping is how kids learn to do these things. My husband's father is a pretty decent mechanic, but my husband knows very little about cars. When he was young and eager to learn, his dad wouldn't let him help out. Dad wasn't being mean; he just was in a hurry to be done, didn't want J.D. to get dirty, wanted the job done just so, or didn't think a kid could really be interested."

Outdoor Activities

A surprisingly large number of the strong families who participated in our research mentioned outdoor activities as favorite ways to be together. Many play catch or yard games. They camp, canoe, hike, picnic, stargaze, play league sports, bicycle, walk, and swim. Their responses give some clues to the allure of the outdoors:

"We love to canoe a little river not far from here. The appeal to me is the beauty of the spot. After a day of sunlight on the leaves, fresh air, the ripple of the water, my soul is refreshed. My husband says he feels more in touch with the eternally important things. He gains perspective; petty trials come and go but the river flows on. The kids have a blast swimming, collecting rocks, hunting fossils, and chasing frogs."

* *

"We have a special town on the Gulf Coast that is a favorite of ours. We camp and fish and go crabbing. There are no phones or television. For a couple of days the outside world disappears. What a pleasure it is to get up when we want, eat when we're hungry, and be free of schedules."

Indoor Recreation

"Every Sunday night we make popcorn and watch a movie on our videodisc player."

* *

"We've enjoyed board games like Monopoly or Scrabble, a walk after dark to look at the stars, telling stories or reading aloud as a change from television."

* *

"We enjoy jigsaw puzzles as a family fun pursuit. The only problem is that it is hard to leave a good puzzle. Once or twice we've lost track of the time until two A.M., so we try to be really careful on school nights."

As you may have assumed, some of our strong families spoke out against television; they feel that television interrupts and demands too much attention. As a result, some have strict limits on the amount of time spent watching, or they have banished the television to the basement to make it less accessible and have sought other leisure pursuits. Others have attempted to improve the time spent watching television. They turn down the volume during commercials and discuss what they've seen. Or they'll discuss the commercials with their children, asking questions like "Is this realistic?" "Do you think [this product] will make you happier, prettier, et cetera?"

Church, Synagogue, School, Et Cetera

For many strong families, weekly worship is a family event. Activities at school, Scouting, or 4-H often involve the entire family as well. If the children have a band concert, recital, or are in a program, Mom and Dad and the family are in the audience.

Special Events

These include holidays, vacations, and personal observances such as birthdays. Members of strong families regard these as times when the entire family should be together. They explain:

"Birthdays are big events at our home. We have a special meal and cake. The birthday person gets presents, of course. We also have added our own twist. The birthday person gives small presents to family members as a way of thanking them for enriching his [her] life."

* *

"Holidays are special times. We enjoy decorating the house, fixing special foods. We have traditions for most holidays — jack-o'-lanterns at Halloween, a food basket to give to a needy family at Thanksgiving, an egg tree at Easter, a trip to the cemetery on Memorial Day."

* *

"Our vacations are planned with everyone in the family in mind. We try to work in antique or craft shops for Mom, some fishing for Dad, and amusement parks or swimming for the children."

THE ULTIMATE SHARING

The Sand Hills are a vast area of grass-covered sand dunes in central and western Nebraska. For miles and miles sand, wind, and sky dominate. The area is used for cattle grazing, but because it takes so much land to support one cow, the ranches are enormous. One woman from the Sand Hills told us about her thirty-seven-year marriage. She and her husband have spent their entire married life on several thousands of acres of short-grass prairie. Their nearest neighbor is ten miles away; the nearest community is fifty miles. To see a movie or buy groceries means a round trip of one hundred miles.

Their life is an almost timeless mix of ranch work, rest, formal worship on Sunday, and an occasional visitor. Sometimes they go several days without seeing anyone but each other. One January blizzard buried them in snow for three weeks before the snow plows dug them out. They told us:

"Most people think we lead a hard and lonely life. That would be true if our situation were different. But we share so much — our love of this open, quiet country, our work making the ranch successful and our special feelings for each other. We're more than married; we're best friends."

While the isolation of the Sand Hills would sound foreign to many of our strong families, the essence of this Sand Hills marriage would seem very familiar. Many of the husbands and wives in the strong families indicate they are intensely bound together; they share all (or nearly all) aspects of their lives with interest and joy. They are mates, lovers, companions, partners, and best friends. Some, like the Sand Hills couple, share even their work as well. The central satisfaction in their lives is their relationship. Many people might think this type of relationship is stifling or phony, but our strong families say this is not so. Their intimacy and sharing are genuine. One California husband's remarks are especially insightful:

"I didn't completely understand this myself until a couple of years ago. My wife's dad was seriously ill, and she went back home to help care for him. For nearly a month we were apart. During that time I managed just fine; I can find my way around the kitchen and laundry room. I was busy at work and still visited friends. I never felt abandoned or terribly lonely.

"The strange thing was that so many things that bring us joy — the theater, sailing, gardening — were *not* the same without her. I went to the theater one evening; I enjoyed the production, but not having her to share it made it sort of ho hum.

"It came to me that the joy of life comes from the two of us together rather than outside things like career, hobbies, or leisure activities. I hope you won't misunderstand: we don't control or monopolize each other; neither one is a parasite. We're capable, independent people who *choose* to be together. And we have more fun that way!"[3]

BABIES DON'T KEEP

"I don't have any idea what I did all day today," she told us with a smile, "but I was busy every second." Indeed she no doubt was. This New Mexico wife and mother has "temporarily retired" from teaching to rear her four children — all under age ten. Her day is a free-flowing whirlwind. Bright and busy children come up to her time and again for support, to show something they have made, to ask for help, or just because they are happy to be with her. Her philosophy is found in an anonymous poem framed on the hallway wall:

> Cleaning and scrubbing
>   Can wait 'til tomorrow,
> For babies grow up,
>   We've learned to our sorrow—
> So quiet down, cobwebs,
>   Dust, go to sleep—
> I'm rocking my baby,
>   And babies don't keep.

Babies don't keep. Neither do older children and marriage relationships! Members of the strong families have learned that it isn't enough to speak of commitment to the family or to plan to show it "someday." They must demonstrate that commitment now. Nowhere is their commitment more clearly demonstrated than in the amount of time they spend together.

RABOOS AND ALLIGATORS

Strong families realize that communication isn't going to be good unless they have some time together. One North Dakota father told us, "My wife understands all the jabber our two-year-old does because the two of them spend lots of time together. Margaret was there when little Lyn named rabbits 'raboos.' Lyn calls alligators 'cup' because she has a drinking cup with an alligator on it. It makes sense when you know the details. It's like that in other areas of communication.

You have to spend time with people to know them and to talk with them to get beyond superficial matters. Some families I know aren't face-to-face long enough each week to discuss football scores and the weather much less get on to matters of heart and mind."

THE BEST GIFT

Most of us spend time and money several times a year selecting perfect gifts for birthdays, anniversaries, or holidays for the people we love. The very best gift of all would take nothing from the bank account. And you wouldn't have to wrap it.

If you believe, like most people, that your life is the most valuable possession you have, then a piece of your life is the most precious gift you have to offer. We give that precious gift in the chunks of our time we give to our loved ones. The families in our research give generously of their lives to each other, and that is one important reason why they are strong families.

PUTTING IT TO WORK

1. Take a journey of happy memories: close your eyes and think back to your childhood, wander through the memories, and bring back the three or four happiest. Could you create some similar experiences for your family? Amie DeFrain remembers winning a pumpkin-decorating contest in 1980 with a two-faced presidential election pumpkin — Jimmy Carter on one side, Ronald Reagan on the other. Naturally she had help: Mom gave technical advice, Dad donated neckties and photographed the end result. She'll never forget that experience.

Nick and David have enjoyed attending University of

Nebraska basketball games as special father-son outings. Eleven-year-old David has decided he wants to attend the university where his dad teaches so they can continue this tradition.

2. Have a "date" with your spouse on a weekly, bi-weekly, or monthly basis. Leave the kids at home. Go out to eat or do something fun. Don't get in a rut; try some new restaurants, try bowling or miniature golf or a moonlight walk around the lake.

3. Let the children help with household chores, but work together. Have them fix salad while you prepare the casserole for dinner. Sort clothes or fold laundry as a team.

4. Set aside 15 minutes when the kids come in from school to share a snack and talk.

5. Designate one wall (or room) in the house for family mementos. Hang pictures of Mom and Dad, the kids, the pets, grandparents, houses you lived in before, favorite vacation spots, etc. Decorate the room with souvenirs of trips — shells from the beach, for example. The room may not win any awards for interior design, but the furnishings will have meaning for your family. A feeling of family identity will be created.

6. Design a family symbol or logo. Have it printed on T-shirts or jackets so that everyone in the family has matching jackets or shirts. Again this fosters family identity.

7. Write down or tape-record your family's history. Involve grandparents and other older relatives. Ask grandparents questions like "What were your parents' (and grandparents') names?" "Where did they live?" "Where are they buried?" "Where did you live as a child?" "What occupations did these folks follow?" "Who are your brothers and sisters?" "How did you and your spouse meet, court, and marry?" "Give the names of your children, when and where they were born." "Where did you attend school?" "How did you celebrate Christmas, Halloween, birthdays, harvests, July 4, as a child?" For the immediate family include infor-

mation about places of residence, circumstances surrounding the birth of each child, vacations, special events, et cetera. Use pictures if possible.

8. Have a family reunion. Make it easy for everyone. Take a potluck picnic to the park. The kids can play while the adults talk. If the family is scattered, a central location is helpful. For example, if your parents live in New Mexico, your in-laws in Wyoming, you're in Nebraska, and other kin are in Utah or Nevada, you might rent a condominium in Colorado for a week of skiing and family reunion.

9. Plan opportunities for one-on-one relationships to grow. For example, Nick occasionally takes David to a movie or to play miniature golf as a twosome; when grandparents visit, Nancy has time alone with her parents or Nick has time with his folks and the grandparents have the boys alone. It gives time for those separate relationships to be cultivated and augments together times.

6

Spiritual Wellness

———————◆❖◆———————

Several years ago, as *Star Wars* was just beginning to make motion picture history, several of the actors in it were surprised to receive letters telling them what an inspiration the movie was. Actors always like fan mail, but these letters were different. Numerous people wrote that *Star Wars* was a spiritual experience for them.

Remember Obi-Wan Kenobi telling young Luke Skywalker about the Force — the unseen, universal link between all people? He told of power in the Force if Luke could only believe, trust, and tap into it. And many people watching the movie were reminded of their own spiritual dimension.

Sometimes we have a hard time talking about the spiritual realm. We're embarrassed or cannot find the right words. And yet over and over again the strong families talked about an unseen power that *can* change lives, *can* give strength to endure the darkest times, *can* provide hope and purpose.

This hidden power — the spiritual dimension of ourselves — is one of the important secrets to the success and strength of the strong families in our research.

What exactly do we mean by the spiritual dimension? Our strong families described it in various ways: faith in God, faith in humanity, ethical behavior, unity with all living things, concern for others, or religion. Our definition must be broad because the strong families are very diverse; their backgrounds differ; their experiences are not the same. And because *religion* is a very touchy subject for many people. In fact, some of you may be ready to go on to the next chapter because you aren't in any mood for a sermon or you don't believe in a higher power. Don't leave just yet. Maybe we can agree on some vital points.

The *Scribner-Bantam English Dictionary*[1] defines spiritual as "non material; of or pertaining to the spirit or soul." Let's focus on the word *soul*. While many persons regard the soul as the immortal part of man or woman, *soul* also describes the part of human nature where feelings, ideas, and morals are centered.

An ancient Buddhist thought is that spirit is the common denominator that we all share and that the spirit alone is permanent and eternal.

We can also agree that humans are multifaceted creatures. We are physical beings with emotional and social sides. We are also creatures of intellect and spirit. Jerry Lafferty, in "A Credo for Wellness,"[2] describes spiritual wellness as encompassing integrity, honesty, loyalty, conscientiousness, virtue, ethics, values, usefulness, self-esteem, and significance.

Spiritual wellness is illustrated by our strong families as a unifying force, a caring center within each person that promotes sharing, love, and compassion for others. It is a force that helps a person transcend self and become part of something larger. This definition is similar to that of some scholars.[3]

For many of our strong families, the yearnings of their

spiritual nature are expressed by membership in an organized religious body such as a church, synagogue, or temple. For many people spirituality manifests itself as concern for others, involvement in worthy causes, or adherence to a moral code.

FAIR WARNING

At the onset of this discussion of strong families and spiritual wellness we need to give you fair warning. We are not going to make any great theological statements about the nature or existence of God. We didn't discuss the specifics of theology, dogma, or creed with our strong families.

And although specific beliefs are reflected in their answers, for the most part it seems that the type of conviction (Christian, Jewish, et cetera) was not as important as the presence of some kind of shared conviction. One midwestern woman said, "I can't imagine sharing my life with a husband who didn't believe in the same things as I do. It would be like living with an alien." And a man from the West Coast summarized the feelings of many strong family members when he said, "Men and women are more than animals; we have spirits or souls. People have to tend to the needs of their spirits just as they feed their physical bodies. Whether you go to church or where you go to church isn't as important as recognizing that people are more than material or physical beings. After all, most religious groups have merit and are usually alike in general beliefs even though they differ in details." And a mother from Georgia said, "I think the critical element for our family is that we *share* a belief in a supreme being and in the basic goodness of people. Religious belief is so important in anyone's life that to find another person who shares it really creates a bond between the two."

What They Gain

For the strong families we have studied, spirituality (spiritual wellness, religion, faith — whatever you wish to call it) is a powerful and important source of strength. That is true because spirituality adds to their lives in several ways.

Purpose or Meaning

"What is life all about?" "Why am I here?" Members of strong families have asked themselves these questions — just as the rest of us have. For many of them the assurance that their lives have purpose comes from their spiritual side.

Several families told us of surviving enormous personal tragedies largely because of this sense of purpose. The story of Ted and Nell is typical. Their life together sounded like a storybook account: happily married for twelve years with two lovely daughters, he advancing in his profession, the family close and loving, enjoying life in a pleasant southern city. Then Nell began having a persistent backache. Several trips to the doctor and extensive testing led to surgery that revealed renal cell carcinoma — a vicious cancer that spreads like wildfire.

They made repeated trips to Houston for cobalt treatments and chemotherapy; they prayed. Nell's gravest concern was that she wouldn't get to rear her girls. Ted and Nell grew closer together, uniting to meet the challenge of her illness. Her physical condition deteriorated; six months after her surgery she passed from this life quietly in her sleep at home. Ted talked about their experience and belief:
"I hoped and prayed for something good to come out of this. I believe there is a God. I believe He is in control. I believe it is in His power to intervene in human disaster. Why He did not intervene for us, I don't know. Life and death are such integral parts of the human condition that we can hardly feel we were unfairly chosen for tragedy. In our twelve years of marriage, we had many good things.

"I still don't know exactly what the purpose of her illness was. I may never have a revelation on why it all happened. The only thing I can think of is that I should not cast all that [Nell's life, illness, death; their closeness; how they met challenge; how their family coped] aside and forget it. It's a part of me. I should try to share what's important about it with other people.

"Our belief in God and that life is eternal was a great comfort and help to both Nell and me throughout this experience. There is an old Oriental poem which has also helped me and I have certainly found it to be true:

> 'Love is the shadow of the evening,
> Which strengthens with the setting sun of life.'

"I guess to love is the highest purpose, and if we do that we can get through anything."

The feeling that our lives are serving a purpose contributes immeasurably to overall satisfaction. Comments from several strong family members attest to this:

"I want to share a negative example with you. I know a young man — twenty years old — who has attempted suicide four times in the last year. He cannot shake off his depression and straighten out his life. He's had some rough times, but no worse than many other people. He's reasonably intelligent and has friends who want to help. His problem is that he lacks a reason to live. He needs to get caught up in something bigger than himself."

* *

"How could a person live if he [she] thought life was without a purpose? Even minor difficulties would be very depressing. Why bother? And what would there be to get excited about?"

A businessman from Texas told us of his search for meaning:

"I started my adult life with a bang, you might say. My parents were moderately well-to-do and gave me a good start in my own business. It flourished, and things looked rosy for ten years or so. Then the economy went sour at about the time I had made some risky investments. One by one those went down the tubes. In the end we lost everything — house, cars, and the business.

"My wife and I sat out by the lake one night and talked until the sun came up. I remember feeling like I had been stripped of everything — like I'd been robbed. 'Why try again?' I asked her. 'We may work and work only to lose it.' We struggled with that a long time. Finally we decided that we had been thinking wrong. The purpose of life isn't to accumulate money, swimming pools, cars, and fur coats. The purpose of life is to enjoy life (because it is a precious gift), to cherish your family and friends, to become a better person intellectually and spiritually, and to help other people. The investments of time and effort I make in family and friends, in charitable work, and in improving myself can never be lost. Things in the mind and heart can't be taken away.

"We did start over again and have enjoyed success. We've replaced many of the material things we lost, but most importantly, we have changed our thoughts. The job, the possessions, the money are no longer an end in themselves. They are a means of making life pleasant and serving others. If I lost them all tomorrow I'd still feel rich."

And a young Arkansas mother spoke to us of her purpose in life:

"I have many ordinary goals just like everyone — pay my bills, rear my kids, have some fun in life. I also have a large objective of working for world peace. I believe one woman *can* make a difference. I speak at various club meetings and I print a small newsletter. We have a small but growing group of supporters. I began this work not very long ago. I was moved by a poem of sorts. It describes the earth as seen from space — a perspective not enjoyed by philosophers and people of peace in the past. It goes like this:

> *'To see the Earth as it truly is,*
> *small and blue and beautiful in that*
> *eternal silence where it floats, is to see*
> *ourselves as riders on the Earth*
> *together, brothers on that bright*
> *loveliness in the eternal cold —*
> *brothers who know now they*
> *are truly brothers.' "* [4]

Positive, Confident Outlook

A belief that life has meaning and purpose helps members of strong families to maintain their perspective. They aren't swamped by temporary troubles. Their outlook on life stays positive and confident. "Our religious beliefs give us a great sense of confidence," says one mother in New England. "We know we are not alone and do not have to depend upon ourselves completely. There is a higher power present."

Joan's ten-year-old son was killed in an accident at a church ice-cream social. She talked to us at length about the people and factors that helped her through that terrible time. She concluded, "One song went over and over in my head; the meaning of the hymn is that God is with me and will help me cope, give me strength. I never ever felt that I couldn't get through. Many people came up to me and said, 'We lost a child, too.' And I'd think, 'Hey, they made it. So can I.' "

Guidelines for Living

When we asked how religion or spiritual wellness contributes to family strength, quite a few families told us they thought the most important way was by providing guidelines for living. A sampling of their answers follows:

"The belief that we are not alone helps us to deal with conflict and anger. We believe we have divine guidance to show us the best way when we disagree."

* *

"We remind ourselves that all living creatures are wonderful and marvelous. That certainly includes humans. So even when they *do* dumb things, they still *are* worthwhile. I love my husband and son even when I don't like what they're doing. That kind of philosophy helps me to be more patient and forgiving.".

* *

"The old, old rule of treating other people as you'd like to be treated just can't be beat as a succinct guide for good relationships."

* *

"Most of the religions I'm familiar with value behaviors that are helpful in creating good family relationships. By that I mean that things like responsibility and concern for others, empathy, love, forgiveness, honesty, controlling anger, gentleness, and patience are all taught as virtues."

Freedom and Peace

Lowell is a pharmacist who was storming through life full speed ahead until a heart attack followed by triple by-pass surgery felled him. He tells about his discovery of freedom:

"Lying there on that hospital bed, I realized one thing, and I just said to myself, 'Well, it's in God's hands now.' And I knew it wasn't just the operation and the doctors and all that — it was *me*. I was in God's hands, and I'll tell you, for a man like me (or like I was then) that's a tough thing to admit. Because, see, I had always thought He wanted me to be in charge, and boy, was I in charge! I was the most *in charge* fellow you ever saw back in those days. And when I had that heart attack it threw me. I couldn't figure out why God let that happen to me when I was trying my best to manage everything He'd given me. I was a pretty good manager, too, if I do say so.

"I'd always felt like everything I had — my friends included, and my family, of course — were direct gifts from God, and then to wind up flat on my back with the doctor telling me I had to slow down and think about letting some other people take care of some of my responsibilities — well, it was a hard thing for me.

"Now when you ask me about my faith, well, it's easy to say I've always been a Christian, at least ever since I was a kid. My folks were practicing Christians; they lived at home the way most people only live on Sundays, and I've tried to raise my family that way too. But I've probably never doubted the presence of Christ in my life as much as I did right after the heart attack. It just didn't make *sense* to me! I thought I knew what I was doing and that I was doing what He had in mind for me.

"During the week after my heart attack and before the bypass surgery I was almost crazy with anger and fear. I had so many plans, and this cheated me out of them. I feared I would die; I'd lie in bed listening to the beep of the heart monitor, wondering how it would be to hear it quit.

"Faith, to me, is what happens when you can't make sense of life yourself. Then you have to wait and God gives you the understanding. At least, He did for me. I guess it took me the better part of a week to realize that what He wanted was for me to hand Him the keys and let Him be boss again.

"And as soon as I surrendered control, I felt a flood of relief — from fear, from anger, from anxiety. I knew with complete confidence that God would care for me — whether I lived or died, whether I went back to work or not. The peace of that realization is enormous."

Lowell has made excellent physical and emotional recovery. He feels better than he has in many years and works a reasonable schedule once again. By tuning in to the spiritual side of himself, Lowell found freedom from fear, anger, and anxiety. He found peace. A Kansas woman told us of her revelation about peace:

"I was having one of those particularly difficult times. Everything seemed to be going wrong at work; my folks weren't doing well healthwise. A routine physical had turned up a lump in my breast. Naturally all I could imagine was cancer.

"Partly to distract myself I went to the shopping center and was meandering through a gift shop when I saw a plaque that said:

> *'Sometimes God stills the storm*
> *To calm His frightened child.*
> *Sometimes He lets the storm rage*
> *And calms His child instead.'*

"I immediately bought it and went home. Two possibilities awaited me — either my troubles would clear up or God would strengthen and quiet me to meet them. Either way I didn't have to worry or be afraid."

Freedom from worry, anger, anxiety, and fear is not the only freedom that religion brings to strong families. Many report a freeing from guilt and low self-esteem.

"I believe that I will be forgiven if I can forgive others. It's like the law of physics about every action having an equal reaction. If I forgive I am forgiven. So I don't have to carry around a load of guilt."

* *

"It sounds contradictory — I think people should strive to improve themselves, but they shouldn't be so hard on themselves either. The way I figure it, I need to do my best to do what I think is right and then not worry or be guilty about it."

* *

"The intrinsic value of each person is such a strong part of my religious belief. I know people make mistakes, but they are valuable anyway. We don't earn God's love, but we must be worthwhile or He wouldn't love us."

* *

"I like the analogy of a human body in thinking about the importance of each person. Each of us has talents and skills. My talent may be less than yours or greater than someone else's. It doesn't matter. We each have a contribution to make. The whole body can't be 'eyes' — some parts have to be 'ears' or 'feet' — and it takes all the parts working together to make the body complete."

Support from Like-minded People

One of the benefits of membership in a religious group is the fellowship and support from people who share beliefs. Ike and Meg in New Mexico get a great deal of pleasure out of their biweekly Bible-study group. The handful of couples gather for a potluck meal (at a different home on a rotating basis) and then have a free-flowing discussion. "Last time we talked about what it means to turn the other cheek," Meg explained.

Besides a lively discussion on an important moral or ethical question, the couples gain the pleasure of a night of "adult" company (a teenager is paid to keep the younger children outside or in another room); they are in the company of other people committed to family and to things of the spirit; the food is good; the laughter is genuine; and it doesn't cost much.

A mother from Tennessee told us of the help she received from people at church:

"This happened a long time ago — fifteen years, I guess, by now. Our family has come a long way since then because of a wonderful group of people. They don't think of themselves as extraordinary and they'd tell you they were only doing what was right. Here's what they did for us.

"My husband and I were married too young and had Jenny too soon. (Hindsight is always clear, you know.) I found myself in a tiny, dingy trailer with a demanding infant. Bill's job kept him away long hours. I didn't have any friends in the community. Alone and overwhelmed, I slipped into a depression. I'd be so depressed I couldn't move; it would take all my effort to change Jen's diaper and stick a bottle of formula in her mouth. I couldn't cook or clean. Bill would bathe Jen and wash diapers and tidy up when he came home, but he couldn't keep up with it. Finally he asked some ladies at the congregation for help.

"Three of the more mature women — grandmothers, all of them — took turns coming to the trailer. They cleaned and cooked, did laundry and took care of Jenny. She needed the rocking and cuddling; they helped me to see that I had to get well to rear her. And I learned a lot of practical stuff by watching how they managed time and paced themselves.

"As soon as I began to feel a tiny bit better, we were invited by another young couple to their home for dinner and cards. I didn't want to go, but everyone insisted. I felt better after. The next week another family had us over for dinner. Soon I felt like I had some friends.

"Someone telephoned every day to see how we were. Ladies stopped by for coffee and conversation or to go shopping. As I improved, the intensive care — the ladies who came over every day — slacked off to let me resume what I could. Eventually they didn't have to come. But the friendships stayed. We are still close to two couples we grew to know during that time. Time and distance separate us now — one couple lives in Dallas, the other in Boston — but we write and telephone and occasionally vacation with each other. We truly are brothers and sisters in spirit."

Other strong family members told us of support and aid from people of their religious community during illnesses, births of babies, deaths, and natural disasters like fires or floods. And even during good times, the contact with like-minded people is a source of encouragement, a reminder of values, and a model for conduct.

FROM THEORY TO PRACTICE

Often we are asked about the practical application of the ideas and ideals of spiritual wellness. As a result, we have talked with our strong families about the "nuts and bolts" of spirituality just as we asked about their communication habits and methods of expressing appreciation. We have asked them, "How do your family members express their spiritual dimension?" and "How do you nurture spiritual wellness in your family?" Their answers fall into four broad categories.

Traditions and Rituals

One of the most apparent demonstrations of the spiritual nature is participation in religious traditions and rituals. Tradition and ritual have been criticized at times as being mechanical and meaningless — empty motion. Certainly that can be the case. But for our strong families, tradition and ritual are outward expressions of a deeper commitment. The following remarks were typical:

"My husband and I have always been active in church functions. It's important to us as a source of renewal and as one way we teach our children."

* *

"We attend worship services each week as a family. We sit together."

* *

"We started a tradition in our family when our children reached junior high and we realized how bad the drug problem was getting in school and how much peer pressure they face each day. We began having family devotionals at breakfast each morning. We felt these established a tone and reminded the children each morning of what we believed."

* *

"The major milestones in our family are marked by religious observances. We were married by a minister in a chapel. Each of our children was blessed and dedicated as an infant; later they were confirmed in the church. We hope they will be married in a religious ceremony. Deaths are noted by funerals conducted by the church."

* *

"Holidays are a good time to reaffirm some of our beliefs, because many holidays are basically religious in origin. Christmas, Easter, Thanksgiving — all have spiritual meaning in our home."

Religious Heritage

"We have a rich spiritual heritage that we rely on for support and guidance. We believe the Bible and other religious literature — stories of spiritual leaders and missionaries, inspirational stories, for example — have timeless truths for living the best way. We've tried to use those to guide our lives."

* *

"A couple years ago we celebrated the Passover meal on our own. We are Christians but felt we would like to tap into some of our religious history. We roasted lamb, made a salad of greens and herbs, and fixed unleavened bread. We told the story of the Israelites in Egyptian slavery, of Moses and the plagues. So many of our symbols — Christ as the sacrificial lamb, deliverance from the bondage of sin, and the unleavened bread of communion — come from then. I feel like an unseen chain binds us back through time and space to those people and events and their beliefs."

* *

"Our children enjoy stories about heroes. We've tried to make sure that the heroes they learn about have traits that make them good models. As a result we rely heavily on Bible characters."

Religious or spiritual history and heritage provide guidelines for living, good models for character development, and a sense of belonging to a larger group. Strong families also indicate an awareness of their spiritual heritage in the celebration of holidays.

Prayer and Meditation

A man in Pennsylvania relates the story of how he and his wife started a family business:

"We opened our business several years ago with little more than a dream and a great deal of faith. We borrowed most of the money to start; the building wasn't much to look at. Some of our friends and relatives didn't think we had a chance of making it. But we hung in there. At first it was just my wife and I working very long hours. Then in a few years we were able to hire part-time help. After a few more years we moved into a new, larger establishment. Sure, there were hard and discouraging times. There were moments when we thought that if we had good sense we would have quit long ago.

"But we didn't quit and the business became very successful."

"What made your business enterprise so successful?" we asked. He indicated that hard work, good judgment, and treating people right were all important factors contributing to their success. But this man declared that the most important influence on the success of the family's business was something else. And he felt this something else also brought them closer together as a family. He relates:

"I believe the most important reason for what you do and the way you feel comes from inside you. So we put together our own simple formula for dealing with problems and overcoming our difficulties, both in our business and in our individual personal lives. We practiced this on a day-to-day basis and it really has worked wonders for us. We highly recommend it.

"The formula is in two words — *pray* and *visualize.* To me prayer is the most effective way of getting in touch with my inner self and of making the connection between myself and the great source of all life and power that we call God.

"For us prayer is a daily practice of talks and meditation with God. We talk to God as a loving friend, not as a distant, unconcerned presence. Most of the prayers are short and we use everyday language — not *thee* and *thou.*

"I start the day with a prayer of praise in the early morning as I jog. We pray as we drive to and from work. We ask God to show us how to deal with a specific situation. We say, for example, 'God, give us your divine guidance and fresh insight in this matter of . . .' Sometimes we pray as a family, but usually it is an individual thing.

"After I have prayed about something I practice visualizing in my mind a good, positive outcome for everyone. I then put it completely in God's hands and I don't worry about it.

"You know, a person's life goes better when that person can get in touch with the resources of wisdom and peace that lie within each one of us. Usually people barely tap those inner resources because they are never still or quiet long enough to do it. Prayer is a way of getting in touch not only with our inner resources but with the unlimited resources of God. Through our prayers we can touch God's great wisdom, love, and peace."

A Texas couple told us, "We join in family prayer each evening. We pray for each other, for guidance for our decisions, and for help with our problems. This puts us on a higher level of thinking and opens new dimensions for us. Our family becomes a circle of power; prayer energizes us."

A man from the Colorado mountains said, "I like to spend some time every day or every other day in meditation or prayer or whatever. I call it 'pondering the wonder' myself. I take a walk in the woods and marvel at the wonder of growing things or the steady progression of the seasons. Golden autumn leaves, the way mushrooms pop up overnight, the songs of birds are all miracles of a sort. Thoughts like that have power to renew my spirit."

And a woman from Mississippi talked to us about meditation:

"I use meditation on a daily basis to flood my mind with positives. I find a quiet, comfortable place and spend several minutes relaxing and clearing my mind. Then I repeat a thought I want to impress. If, for example, I'm in conflict with someone at work, I may repeat, 'We are both part of humanity; we can resolve the conflict.' Then I spend some more time in quiet contemplation. I end the meditation feeling refreshed and relaxed."

Various controlled studies in laboratory settings have monitored the effects of meditation and prayer. They reveal that many persons experience a lowering of blood pressure, a movement to higher-level brain-wave activity, and a heightened sense of peace and well-being. These results confirm what our strong families have told us about prayer and meditation.

Everyday Life

All the talk of religious belief, spiritual heritage, faith, and whatever would be only empty talk were it not for the fact that for our strong families, the primary expression of their spiritual dimension is in everyday life. They literally practice what they preach.

Many report an awareness of a divine Presence in their lives. Their comments help us to understand:

"I talk to God as I would to a friend, for I feel He is always near."

* *

"I believe that a divine Being is always present, guiding my life in ways that are best for me."

* *

"You know you're not alone. A great strength and power is present. We tie into that power through prayer and meditation."

Spiritual wellness is a very personal, practical, day-to-day matter for the strong family members. Religion is neither superficial ritual nor highly theoretical theology. Again, their statements give insight into the meaning of this:

"We are committed to a spiritual life-style — a livable rather than theoretical religion. Maybe that's because we're practical people by nature. If it doesn't apply in daily life, what use is it?

"The beauty is that so many of our religious teachings are very practical if you only give them a chance. Take, for example, the teaching that when we are angry we are not to sin. We aren't told not to get angry; that's very unrealistic. We are told to manage the anger, and that's excellent advice. Temper tantrums, unresolved resentment, and uncontrolled conflict can be very damaging to the individual and to relationships."

* *

"Our family has certain values: honesty, responsibility, and tolerance, to name a few. But we have to practice those in everyday life. I can't talk about honesty and cheat on my income tax return. I can't yell responsibility and turn my back on a neighbor who needs help. I'd know I was a hypocrite, and so would the kids and everyone else."

* *

"Among many Native American peoples in the Southwest, a person is not considered dead until all those who have known him [her] are also dead. As long as someone remembers, that person is among the 'living dead.' That idea has given me much comfort.

"My mother died when I was a teenager. Dad has done a wonderful job with my brothers and me, but I miss my mom. I hate it that she isn't here for special times like graduation and my engagement. So I visit the cemetery often to 'talk' with her. I straighten up the grave site and then sit and tell her about my life, my troubles, my joys. Sometimes I cry; sometimes I laugh. Without fail, I leave feeling better.

"Some people would think I'm crazy, I suppose. But my mother is still alive in my heart and she's still an important part of my life — always will be."

* *

"The most recent conversation in our house has been about our television watching habits. We — as a family — are evaluating how much we watch and what we watch. If a half-minute commercial can convince us to buy a certain toothpaste or cereal, doesn't it seem logical that a whole show can convince us to buy certain habits? We don't condone excessive drinking, marital infidelity, casual premarital sex, smoking, or violence. What influence does it have on our lives to watch all that on TV? I don't mean to get on a soapbox there, but this is a good example of how we try to apply our spiritual values to real life."

* *

"I believe that there is goodness and greatness in each individual. Each of us is a tiny drop of water in the ocean of humankind. Believing that, I have to strive for causes that benefit humanity: ending world hunger, finding global peace, preserving our planet's environment."

ALL YOU NEED

Earlier in this chapter we shared some of the thoughts of Joan, whose ten-year-old son was killed in an accident at an ice-cream social. Her husband, Bruce, is a minister, and the death of their son was a severe trial and torment to him. He reread all his old funeral sermons, searching for solace over Andy's death. Finding no satisfactory answers, he returned to Chicago, where he had attended seminary years before. He spent long hours with his mentors, the men who had helped him become a minister. "There is no answer to the question of why Andy died," they told him. "God is with you. That is all you need. The real agony — the real wilderness — is not pain or suffering or disappointment or even death. The real agony is the absence of God."

Members of our strong families would agree: the challenges and trials of life are bearable and surmountable because of the spiritual resources they can tap. Without the spiritual dimension to give lasting meaning, life would lack purpose and direction; they would suffer alienation and depression. Instead they feel a part of something bigger than self (a part of an eternal spirit or of humanity) and that gives them perspective, hope, optimism, and confidence.

Sustained by their faith in a divine power and in humanity, members of strong families find themselves renewed by acts of kindness and the support of others. Freed from the burden of low self-esteem, they can redefine themselves and their possibilities. With guilt and anxiety removed, they can be loving, open, accepting, and forgiving with others.

The strong families we studied represent numerous religious denominations. The details of each of these faiths are quite divergent. But common themes united all of these people, whether they were Catholic, Protestant, Baha'i, Jewish, Unitarian-Universalist, or had no formal religious affiliation: hope, love, family, an elevation of spirit, a reverence for life, and a sense of the sacred.

In their reverent dealings with each other in their homes, at work, at play, and even in church and synagogue, members of strong families express their spiritual nature — their religion. This brings love, security, purpose, and peace. That is all they need.

PUTTING IT TO WORK

1. Set aside 15–30 minutes each day for meditation, prayer, or contemplation. Take a walk to get away from phones and interruptions; enjoy the beauty of nature. The outdoors and spiritual wellness are clearly linked in the hearts of many strong families. John Muir, father of our National Parks, also held nature in a religious awe. He once explained why he preferred the verb *saunter* over the word *hike:* "You know, when the pilgrims were going from England to the Holy Land, the French would ask them, 'Where are you going?' and they did not speak French very well, but they would say, 'Sante Terre' [Holy Land]. That is where we get our word saunter. . . ."[5]

2. Join a discussion group (or form one with your friends) to consider religious topics, value-related matters, or philosophical issues.

3. Examine your own values and philosophy of life. How do you respond, because of your particular values, to contemporary issues such as abortion versus right to life, capital punishment, or cohabitation? Try keeping a journal of your thoughts and impressions.

4. Help your children to clarify their values. What is most important in life? Work, health, money, popularity? Help them to gain perspective (e.g., the world isn't over because he or she doesn't have a date this weekend).

5. Identify three of your weaknesses (lack of patience, no temper control, worrying too much, et cetera). Decide how to improve in these areas and put your plan to work. Select three of your strengths (neighborliness, compassion, honesty)

and make a conscious effort to develop the traits more fully.

6. Have family devotionals on a regular basis. Read Bible stories or other inspirational material, pray, sing, count your blessings, reaffirm your love and commitment to each other. Keep devotionals short and varied so that the interest of children is stimulated rather than squelched.

7. Volunteer your time and muscle and money to a cause: ending world hunger, peace on earth, helping the disabled, rearing orphans, aiding victims of natural disasters, preventing child abuse and neglect.

7

Coping with Crises
and Stress

———— ◆ ————

A DEADLY GAME

It was a good basketball game. Exciting and fast paced. Well, as fast paced as you could expect for a group of university professors. This was just one of many pleasures Richard enjoyed in his life at the university. He ran up and down the court with no serious concerns on his mind. Life was good; he loved teaching, his family was close and happy, his health was excellent. Then it happened! As one of his teammates shot the ball, Richard prepared to rebound. However, because he had turned his back he did not see the opposing player who also leaped for the ball. They came down hard, the opposing player's elbow digging into Richard's lower back.

His back hurt and was sore for several days. Richard wasn't overly worried. He'd had athletic injuries before and expected as much. But the soreness did not leave; it became worse. The pain became excruciating; dizziness and weakness began to plague him. A long series of hospital visits and medical tests followed. Finally the diagnosis came — a rare disease of the pancreas, triggered by the blow to the back. "I thought knowing what the problem was would help us treat it," said Richard. "What a mistake that was! I learned my condition was disabling and practically always terminal. Life expectancy was less than two years. And most doctors had never seen the condition in practice, so they didn't know what to do with me."

Richard and his wife, Emily, felt as if their world had come to a sudden stop. Their feelings ran the gamut. Total disbelief. Denial. Anger. Deep depression and despair. Piercing fear. What would this do to their lives? How would it influence the lives of their three small sons? What would they do? What could they do?

The first thing they did was to find the very best medical help available for this disease. That took them to the Mayo Clinic. Although Richard received the best medical care, the prognosis was no better. One physician told him, "We're doing all that we can possibly do. But your hope really rests with a Higher Power."

A devout church member, Richard began to pray as never before. "I prayed several times a day," he said. "I also flooded my mind with passages from the Bible. I would read them and meditate upon their meaning. Luke 18:27 was a favorite: 'The things which are impossible with men are possible with God.' "

Things really looked impossible for Richard and his family for the next six years. Three times he had major surgery; twice he almost died. He was hospitalized repeatedly for infections, pneumonia, liver failure, and reactions to medication. Scarcely a month passed without a hospital stay.

Pain was a constant companion, frequently so bad he could not sleep for days. The removal of his pancreas induced diabetes and caused a total metabolic upheaval. He had digestive disturbances and difficulty regulating his blood sugar levels.

Naturally he could not continue a normal work schedule;

the university dismissed him. Disability payments were only about half of what his salary had been, so Emily opened a day-care center in their home. That way she could care for her own sons and Richard and supplement their income.

Still the financial burden was overwhelming. Hospital bills were enormous; Richard required medication on a constant basis. They made repeated trips to the Mayo Clinic. Emily recalled, "People would talk about how fortunate we were to have medical insurance because it paid eighty percent of our bills. And that is fortunate, but they didn't stop to think that we had to pay the twenty percent, and twenty percent of one hundred fifty thousand dollars is a large chunk of money. Richard's bills went over one hundred fifty thousand, even."

Richard and Emily shared their story with us some twelve years after that fateful basketball game. According to the best medical thought, he should have been dead for a decade. No one would have been surprised if he and Emily had divorced and the boys had run amok! Many would not have predicted their survival through such a long-term crisis. And yet Richard is alive and has improved enough that he can work for short periods of time. He is happy and enthusiastic about life. The relationship between him and his sons is close and loving; the boys are growing into fine young men. He and Emily have a very solid marriage. She has moved on to a better-paying job. They know that all of their problems aren't over. Life doesn't work that way. They do know they can face whatever comes along.

How They Survived

We've left some of the story about Richard and Emily untold at this point; we'll tell more later. We opened with their story because it is an inspiration to others and reflects so well how strong families in our research typically responded to crises.

We have identified six strategies used by strong families in crisis situations. Of course, not every family in a crisis will use all six, but in general these are the kinds of action taken by strong families.

Thorns and Roses

A primary factor in the survival of strong families is their ability to see something positive in the situation and to focus on that positive element. Richard talked about this:

"Emily and the children kept my spirits up and probably prevented me from madness by regularly calling attention to our blessings.

"No matter how bad we felt, at each meal we all would mention one thing we were really thankful for and appreciated about our life together. I remember one day our six-year-old said something that had enormous impact on me.

"He said, 'I'm so happy Daddy is with us more now than he used to be.' I later thought, well this is an opportunity to spend time with the children. Why not feel good about it and take advantage of it?"

Paul and Carol out in Portland, Oregon, are good examples too. Paul has a congenital inner-ear problem, which affects his hearing and his balance. The problem got so bad a few years ago that Paul would become nauseated and the world would turn end-over-end. The balance mechanisms of his inner ear were out of whack and the vertigo was becoming a terrible embarrassment. Speaking in front of large audiences in his job as an educator for the county schools, he often felt queasy and dizzy. Embarrassment turned to fear. On the way to work one morning the vertigo came without warning. The street tumbled over and over on itself and he crashed into a barricade in a Safeway parking lot.

A year and two operations later the prognosis was still unclear. Would he need another operation; would he ever be better? The doctors were not hazarding a guess at this juncture. But before this crisis would be resolved another one hit the family. Hard.

Budget cuts hit their county school system. Paul was out of a job. Twice Paul had earned Outstanding Educator awards in his state. Now he would be walking the pavement looking for work; if, that is, he could walk in spite of his vertigo.

Paul and Carol no doubt spent time bemoaning their fate. But they ended up reframing the situation.

"Aren't you depressed?" we asked him.

"Nope."

"Oh, come on. Don't give us that false-bravado stuff!"

"Nope. This may sound silly, but like Carol says, it's a good time to move on. I've been in education twenty years, and this will be the impetus to try something new.

"So I will get out of my rut. I don't know. A blind man down the street became a millionaire selling Tupperware or something over the phone. I won't sell Tupperware, but I have been selling education for twenty years. I've been operating on my mouth. I will continue.

"Carol is really getting into her career. She is doing a bang-up job for the church now. She is chartering a plane to fly a group to the state meeting which she put together. There will be eight hundred people there and she will introduce her group and . . .

"And in twenty years of education I never got to charter a plane!" Paul was seeing strength in Carol he never knew existed. He was full of pride and love for her.

"You know — " he paused in his rapid-fire delivery. "You know, we are stronger now than ever. This is about the worst thing that has happened to us in twenty-one years of marriage. And yet we really love each other.

"The kids are pulling together with us like never before. We are all in this together. We are going to make it. It is really, really fine."

Now please don't get us wrong on this point. We are not the Pollyanna Brothers merrily dancing a jig while the world goes up in flames. Nor are strong families like ostriches with their heads in the sand. They suffer as many serious crises as other families; they cry, get angry, and are depressed. But they are not overwhelmed by crisis and tragedy partly because they manage to see some good coming out of the situation. Their ability to see something good in a crisis or bad situation helps them to maintain a more balanced perspective; it prevents them from becoming so depressed and despondent that they cannot function. In other words, the ability to see something positive in a bad situation gives them hope! Some of their insights follow:

"My brother died suddenly last fall; he was forty-three. After the initial shock and grief, I did some looking into my own life. I guess you could say I asked myself, 'What if I only make it to forty-three?' I've made some financial arrangements so that my young children are better protected if I die early, and I feel good about that. I also have a renewed appreciation for how precious each day of life is. I try not to waste a single day."

* *

"I don't recommend that you burn the house to learn this lesson, but we did stand together in our front lawn one frosty fall morning and looked at the pile of ashes that had been our home. And then we all looked at each other and suddenly we were hugging and crying with joy because *we* were OK. And we are what's most important to each other."

* *

"The hard times in our lives have been good in that they have taught us important things about ourselves. We've learned that we are tough, that we can work together to meet difficulties, that we're survivors.

"I saw a poster that sums up what we've been talking about. It said:

'Roses have thorns or
Thorns have roses.
How do you see life?' "

Pull Together

Members of strong families unite to face the challenges of a crisis. The question they ask is not "What needs to be done?" Sometimes the task is enormous. Nobody could do it alone. The question is "What can *I* do?" Strong family members focus on the small things they can do as individuals to help. No individual feels total responsibility for the problem. Nobody carries the load alone. They all shoulder it.

Emily and Carol, as mentioned earlier, took jobs to ease financial burdens. Children may help with household chores, yard work, or answering the phone. Each family member is a support — physical and emotional — to the others. Some examples help to show how this works.

Pat received a large promotion several months ago. It made her the woman with the highest management-level position in her company, and she regarded it with mixed emotions. She was delighted to advance, but felt a tremendous pressure to do well, not only for herself but for other women employees. It was a crisis because it required a dramatic change in her life-style. Her husband, Ed, and their teen daughter, Becky, pitched in to help. Becky agreed to handle laundry and kitchen cleanup to give Mom time to do reports at home. "Ed has been a sounding board for ideas and has been my 'counselor' when I needed to pour out fears and anxieties. Just someone to listen is so important," said Pat. Ed laughed. "Yes, and I started something I could hardly afford. At the end of her first week in the new position I sent her a single rose; the next week I sent two as a way of saying 'You made it another week.' When we got to a dozen we agreed to quit. She felt confident enough not to need that extra little pat on the back. Maybe I should have picked cheaper flowers, huh?"

Jeff and Linda bought a lovely home near a little creek. As far as anyone knew, the creek had never been out of its banks. Last summer their town received a six-inch-in-a-two-hour-period rain. The flood waters were four feet deep in their living room. Neither was hurt, but they lost all their furniture and appliances, and many personal belongings were ruined. Both of their families helped them. Her parents, who live nearby, gave them a place to stay. His brother and sister gave time and muscle to clean up mud and trash. Dens, basements, and attics have yielded "extras": bed, table, refrigerator, chairs, lamps, and linens. Because the family members pulled together, Jeff and Linda made it through this difficult time.

Other families told us how they joined in to help each other during crises:

"My mom has spent a lot of time with us at the births of our children. She cooks and cleans, tends the older kids, and generally gives me a chance to rest and get back to full force."

* *

"Several years ago my mother was dying. She'd fought a long and courageous battle with cancer but was losing. She was confined to bed and needed lots of care. Our daughter came home to help out — with nursing chores and with decisions like should we put Mom in a nursing home and with details like figuring out Medicare and health insurance claims."

* *

"My brother helped to pull me through a serious illness several years ago. He's not a physician, but he gave me medicine for my spirit. We're from Texas and you know how proud Texans are just to be Texans. He said to me over and over, 'Jim, you're just like a Texas longhorn — mean and tough and not too pretty.' You know, longhorns aren't much to look at, but they are noted for being tough and they survive where other cattle cannot. Soon I found myself thinking, 'Yeah, I'm tough.' "

Go Get Help

Family members — spouse, children, parents, siblings — provide much of the help that a family needs to make it through a crisis. Fortunately, most families don't have to make it alone. And the strong families are smart enough to seek out valuable support from others — their church or synagogue, friends, neighbors, and professionals. Richard and Emily received much help from their church, friends, and neighbors. Countless hours of child care were given by friends and neighbors during Richard's many hospital visits so that Emily might be with him. Food was brought in during difficult times. Their congregation bought airplane tickets for one of their trips to the Mayo Clinic and arranged for Emily to stay with a family in Rochester during Richard's hospitalization there. An "anonymous friend" paid the tuition so their son could continue his music lessons.

An Oklahoma man told us: "Three friends were particularly helpful to me following the death of my wife. One lady came to the house immediately; she tidied up the living room and cleared the refrigerator because she knew people would be coming by to visit and bringing food. Then she fixed the guest room because she knew some relatives from out of town would be coming. She stayed at the house all day taking calls, keeping a record of who brought what so I could write thank-you notes later. She made coffee for the folks who dropped by to pay their respects. I was in no shape to handle all that plus the funeral arrangements.

"Her husband picked up my relatives at the airport and later drove them to the funeral home. They both provided long-term support to me in terms of visiting, having me in their home, and showing they were concerned.

"The third friend is an older lady, a widow. She went

with me to make funeral arrangements and to select a cemetery lot. She, too, was there when I needed her for years after my wife's death."

Another couple explained how they sought professional help: "We had had financial difficulties coming on for quite some time. Farming just isn't that profitable. And then we had record-breaking bad weather for several years and lost most of our crops. Too many years when outgo exceeded income caught up with us.

"We didn't even know where to begin, so we talked with a lawyer and a financial counselor. Bankruptcy is one of our options, and while it isn't a pleasant procedure, it isn't as bad as we thought. But the financial counselor helped us see some other ways to get some cash flowing again. We aren't going to be rich, but we will make it through."

"The worst crisis I've come through," Doris told us, "was the breakup of my first marriage. [Remember, we have talked with strong remarried families as well as first-marriage families.] I had been like many people, lulled into thinking that my spouse was as perfectly content as I. When he came home one night muttering something vague about 'needing a change, needing to grow, needing to be free,' I chuckled in disbelief. It sounded too much like a soap opera.

"His malaise never dissipated, though, and in a month he was gone. As it turned out, he never came back.

"There I was with four young children, no job, and not much education. I cried for about three solid days. Then some friends began to help me pick up the pieces.

"My closest friend volunteered to keep the kids while I went job hunting. Another, who had just begun job hunting herself, gave me tips on interviewing and writing a résumé.

"Our neighbor who teaches at the university talked with me about the possibility of going to college. He brought me a catalogue and enrollment forms.

"I've a network of five friends who counsel and console

me. If one is not at home, I call another. Two of them are professionals: one at the university and one at the community mental health center.

"But, they all help me. And if I have a really tough problem, I call four or five of them in a row. I tell my sad story and they listen and offer suggestions, and then I make a decision."

Use Spiritual Resources

In the previous chapter we learned about the spiritual dimension in the lives of strong families and how important it is to them. It is not surprising then that they draw on those spiritual resources in times of crises, just as they draw on physical resources of energy and muscle and emotional resources of family commitment and concern.

Many find their faith in God's help and guidance to be a powerful force in dealing with the crisis. Remember Richard found peace and hope in prayer and in Bible reading. Look back at the chapter on spiritual wellness and note how many of the families talked about religious faith during crises.

Spiritual beliefs are helpful in crises by providing a philosophy of life, by giving perspective, and by giving hope and comfort. Several strong family members shared ideas like the following:

"Certain things are inevitable. Unless a person dies very young, you're going to experience death, disappointment, grief, illness. That sounds pessimistic if I stop now. Good things like new babies, weddings, promotions, and healing are part of life, too. That puts life in perspective."

* *

"In medieval times people believed in the Wheel of Fortune. We are all riders on the Wheel, and it is constantly turning. When you're at the top of the Wheel of Fortune, life smiles upon you. It is good. But the Wheel is turning, and sooner or later something will happen and you will be upside-down at the bottom. If you cannot hang on tight, you will tumble into the void. The important thing to remember when things are going bad is that if you can hold on just a bit longer the Wheel will turn and life will again be good. That idea has helped me to hang in there through the bad times."

* *

"I dreamed about my father shortly after he died, but the dream had a quality about it that wasn't like an ordinary dream. He said he'd come to give me two pieces of information; one was how to solve a problem with some calves of his. He always bought eight or ten calves each year, raised them, and sold them for beef. The other was about a tax problem with his estate.

"After he told me these two ideas I asked him if he knew he had passed on from this life. I didn't want to say 'Do you know you're dead?' That seemed absurd and rude. He said he did and that everything was fine.

"That dream — if it was a dream — has been a source of comfort to me. I feel like Dad's spirit stayed long enough to help us and maybe he's still not so very far away. By the way, both ideas worked beautifully."

Open Channels

Another reserve that strong families draw upon in times of crisis is their skill in communication. One benefit of open communication channels is that problem solving is made easier. A mother from Colorado said, "As the time of our youngest daughter's wedding approached, I called a family council. Things were getting out of control. Weddings have a way of growing — more guests, more food, more flowers, et cetera. We just couldn't afford the size this one was gaining. And I was feeling very anxious about getting all the arrangements made; I felt swamped. I wasn't employed outside the home when our older daughter was married, so I was able to do more then.

"Our daughter — the bride-to-be — was relieved to be

able to simplify the wedding. We decided to have a less elaborate reception to reduce costs considerably. My husband suggested letting his mother do the flowers. She's done flower arranging for years as a hobby and is quite talented. My husband also volunteered to line up the photographer and musicians.

"Both my husband and daughter were quite willing to help. They hadn't realized how near an anxiety attack I was. We all felt better to get our plan of attack formalized."

A second very important benefit of open communication is that it allows family members to express feelings freely. Crises are times of change and uncertainty; persons caught up in them may feel loss (of health or a loved one), anger, fear, anxiety, and guilt. Being able to express these feelings is a step toward surviving the crisis.

One young man we talked with is an accomplished pilot. He had become concerned when his father, a high-powered, go-go, Type-A-personality lawyer, decided to learn to fly to make professional travel simpler. He continues the story, "Dad took a few lessons and was certified competent. I had my doubts; in fact, I was horrified when I went up with him. But he was always too expert, too professional, too cool around me. I couldn't argue with him. So, I made a joke. I said, 'If you are going to fly, you better get a lot of insurance, because you're terrible. You're going to kill yourself. Ha Ha Ha.'

"Some joke. A few weeks later he went out to practice his new skills. I wanted to go up with him because he was so awful, but my wife and I had planned to go to Sioux Falls to visit her sister and brother-in-law. We hadn't seen them in several years.

"Of course, it happened. Dad crashed and was killed instantly.

"For some time I was obsessed with guilt and anger: anger at him for going, guilt that I didn't go with him. My wife and I spent many hours talking it out. Time after time she's said, 'You didn't know what was going to happen. He was certified to fly, so someone thought he was OK in the air. It was *his* decision to fly — not yours!'

"My brother told me to ease off on blaming myself. He said, 'Dad's always been bullheaded. And he was a grown man capable of making choices. If he chose not to listen to you, that's his fault. I love him as much as you do, but that doesn't change how stubborn he was.'

"Without their help I would have sunk into a terrible stew of anger, guilt, and depression. And I might not have gotten that help if I hadn't told them how I felt."

Go with the Flow

Richard learned to cook and clean and operate the washing machine when Emily went to work. "We traded places," he said; "she couldn't do everything, and I felt more useful, too." Emily learned to think of herself as the family breadwinner. Richard later found work on a part-time basis as an educational consultant; he made a career change. Other families told us similar stories of men and women learning new tasks and roles. Paul in Portland also had to change careers because of his vertigo. Doris went back to college to train for a job.

Charles Darwin, in his discussion of the survival of a species, concluded that only the fittest survive. We have come to believe that one important quality of the "fittest" in any species is adaptability.

A final characteristic of strong families that allows them to weather the storms of life is their adaptability or flexibility. Remember the proverb about the mighty oak so tall and firm that breaks in the strong wind while the fragile-looking reeds bend to the ground but do not snap? Strong families tend to be like the reeds. They bend, they change, they adapt, and when the storm is over they're still intact.

Edna told us about her husband's retirement: "We thought retirement was a reward for years of hard work. No one hinted at how hard we'd have to work at retiring.

"We can laugh about that now, but we had some tricky adjustments to make. All the hoopla leading up to retirement — parties and gifts. And then you wake up one morning and wonder, 'Now what?'

"It didn't take Roger long to catch up on sleeping late, his reading, and television sports. Soon he was hanging around watching me do housework. Then he began offering advice, and that was too much for me!

"We worked out a new style of living that suits us; it took some time, but we kept at it. For one thing, we have a general schedule we follow. We aren't clock-watchers, but we feel less aimless this way. We have breakfast about eight and do house and yard chores until lunchtime. We work together on chores; Roger especially likes to cook. One day a week we go to town, go to the bank and post office, run errands, get groceries and supplies. We have lunch in town on that day.

"Our afternoons are varied. I volunteer at the hospital two afternoons a week and take a craft class one other day. Roger never had time for volunteer work during his employed years. He has become active in county and state politics; he had a wonderful time working for his favorite candidates during the last elections. During slack times he likes to work on his stamp and coin collections.

"We make a point of visiting with friends at least one evening a week — either at their homes or in ours. We all like cards or board games. Roger and I go out on a regular basis on a kind of 'date' — to a movie, concert, or the theater.

"We had to decide how to structure our time; we had to adapt to more free time and more time together. We changed the way we divided household chores. If we hadn't been able to make those changes, we'd have been pretty miserable."

LIKE A BANK ACCOUNT

We're sure you noticed as you read through the characteristics of strong families that help them to cope with crises that we've talked about a couple of them before. Entire chapters have been devoted to *spiritual wellness* and to *communication*. It isn't too hard to see family willingness to pull together as an expression of their *commitment* to each other.

In short, the strengths of these families serve as a pool of resources that they draw on when times are difficult — rather like we save money for a "rainy day." In contrast, unhealthy families are worn out and depleted on a daily basis by the stress of poor relationships.[1] When a crisis comes along, the unhealthy family must add it to the burden they already struggle with. No wonder the extra load is sometimes too much.

THE GREAT GRAY KILLER

To this point in this chapter we have focused on how strong families cope with crises — those major upheavals in life: death, serious illness, loss of a job, a big promotion, retirement, a wedding, divorce, flood, or fire, to name a few. What about the less serious events that cause distress?

People who aren't necessarily in a crisis may nonetheless be suffering from the stress and strain of daily life. Listen to what some families said:

"We've been overdrawn at the bank for the last four months. Our expenses have just been larger than usual. We aren't to the point of bankruptcy or welfare, but getting our budget back on course is a challenge."

* *

"The car decided to quit this week. It had to be hauled in to the garage for repairs. In the meantime, I'm having lots of 'fun' getting rides for the kids and learning bus schedules. What a hassle!"

* *

"I love the winter holiday season, but sometimes I wish it could be more serene. Everyone has parties and there are gifts to buy and wrap and special foods to prepare. I get worn out before it's over, and that's too bad."

These are only a few examples. Each of you could add to the list. Stress comes in many shapes and sizes, and each of us experiences stress on a daily basis.

Stress is not new, although our understanding of it has grown in recent years. Our ancestor who encountered a bear or lion while foraging for food experienced stress. Adrenaline was released; his blood pressure surged; his heart beat faster. He was ready to run faster or fight better as a result. Those same reactions take place in our bodies today when we end up in a traffic jam or the boss snarls or a deadline draws near. Unfortunately those situations don't require "fight or flight." We experience the strong physical and emotional reactions to stress without an effective way of releasing them.

After months or years of such distress, we feel the effects. Medical science has much evidence that the accumulated effects of stress are important factors in heart disease, angina, arrhythmia, hypertension, migraine headaches, ulcers, diabetes, and other diseases, including possibly cancer.

Stress takes its toll in a subtle but deadly way. That is why we call it the great gray killer of our time.

NOW FOR THE GOOD NEWS

That's the bad news: stress can kill us, and it's with us every day; we can't get away from it. The good news is that we don't have to succumb to stress. We can take action to manage the stress we encounter. Our strong families have discovered some important insights into dealing with stress that have proved successful for them.

Keep Things in Perspective

One of the most important things strong families do to minimize stress in their lives is to keep things in perspective. One way of doing this is to realize that stress is a normal part of life. James Taylor sings that everybody has the blues, and our strong families would agree. Several told us:

"Everyone has difficult times. Who doesn't have those days when you get a parking ticket and the boss is cross and traffic snarls and the neighbor's dog gets in your trash cans and it rains and the washing machine blows up — you name it. I try to remember that I have plenty of company in misery. That helps me get through."

Knowing we aren't unique gives us courage and a little more enthusiasm for tackling our troubles head-on. Sometimes we realize our problems aren't so big. One woman told us about her experience on perspective:

"One day I was feeling really pressed and depressed. We had guests coming for dinner, the house was messy, and I resented having to cook and clean. As I washed dishes, I suddenly remembered a young woman we knew. She was gravely ill and too weak to get out of bed. We knew she didn't have long to live. The idea flashed in my mind 'What would she give to have this "awful" day of mine? How happy she'd feel to be able to be up cooking and cleaning or any number of ordinary things.' "

Humor Yourself

The strong families we talked with prescribed humor as an antidote for stress. "Learn to laugh at the crazy things that happen and at yourself," they told us.

A Massachusetts husband said:

"I'm a true fan of M*A*S*H. We get the reruns every evening. I have some of the episodes memorized, but enjoy them all. There's always something that strikes me as funny, and I've thought many times about the way the characters use humor to ease the strain. So many of the situations are like everyday life — not the war part but the problems with other people, the red tape, the weather, loneliness, et cetera."

A New Mexico woman said:

"We try to treat things seriously that need it and poke fun at the rest. We often ask ourselves, 'Will this be funny later?' and lots of petty irritants are. I'll give you an example. We headed out for a company potluck dinner one evening — in a bit of a fluster because we were about five minutes late and my husband was supposed to give the invocation. At the trunk, juggling keys and a casserole, he spilled the hot casserole on his hand and down his trousers. He flipped it onto the lawn (killing the grass, by the way) and raced back inside to change clothes. We raced off and were halfway there when a police officer pulled us over. We had missed a new no-left-turn sign at an intersection. Of course the officer wanted to see my husband's license and you know where his wallet was? Right! At home in the other trousers. There we sat explaining spilled casseroles and changed clothes to the officer. She let us go with a warning. No one would have made up a story like ours. We arrived at the dinner and my husband said, 'I'm sorry we're late but I am *very* thankful just to be here. Let me tell you why. . . .' His humor changed a blood-pressure-raising series of incidents into a good story."

One final example comes from our friend Sally, a courageous woman who was born with a rare degenerative disease that slowly constricts her body. She spends her time in a wheelchair and was in danger of dying when we talked with her. Her spine had bent so much that she was down to thirty percent of her normal breathing capacity. She was slowly suffocating.

A major operation was her only hope; her back would be cut open from top to bottom, and stainless steel inserts put into each vertebra would help straighten her spine. "Normal" life in which one walks and runs would never be possible, but life itself would be possible.

As we talked she joked about being a "bionic woman" and predicted she'd need a whole new wardrobe. We asked why new clothes and she said, "Because I'll be six-foot-seven with all those metal spacers in me. And think what havoc I'll cause in airport metal detectors!"

We asked her, "Seriously, Sally, how can you laugh so much about this?"

"You know what they say," she replied. "It's either laugh or cry."

And laughter often is the balm we need for the silliness, madness, and ironies of daily life.

One Step at a Time

"I divide my work up into small segments and I just work on one segment at a time concentrating only on that. I don't think about the rest of it. That way I don't feel pressured. As a bonus I have a sense of accomplishment when each segment is done."

* *

"Think of it as living in day-tight compartments. If you think about what you have to do in the next week or month you can be overwhelmed and exhausted. If you concentrate on today only, you can usually manage."

These quotations reflect another way strong family members keep stress levels from skyrocketing. They focus on *one* step, *one* task, *one* day at a time.

Give Up Worrying

One highly successful oil man from Oklahoma, a member of a strong family, summarized the responses of many other strong families when he said:

"I used to worry a lot; in my business it's easy to do. It got to the point it was about to break me. Then somehow a very important thing happened to me and I don't know exactly how it happened. I finally realized deep within myself that it was not possible for me to control every little aspect of my life as well as the lives of others, as I had been trying to do. I decided that I could do the best that I could do, but then I had to let go. I had to trust more in other people and in life. I can't do everything on my own; I can't carry the world on my shoulders. This realization gave me an indescribable feeling of relief. I'm a much more relaxed, effective, and productive person."

Worry has been likened to a rocking chair — you make a lot of motion but don't go anywhere. Worry depletes energy, keeps us fearful, and interferes with our effective functioning. One woman who talked to us said:

"I don't say I'm not concerned about things; I still make plans and am careful but I've quit worrying things to shreds. I used to go through two routines: 'what if' and 'if only.' 'If only I hadn't said . . .,' 'If only I had . . .,' 'If only I were . . .,' and 'What if it (rains, snows, freezes, is too hot)?' 'What if it won't work?' 'What if they hate me?' and on and on. I was always miserable.

"A friend suggested I write down a list of worries each week. Then I could sketch out what to do about each. I liked that approach, but the real shock came when I looked back at my list several months later. Had I really *worried* about those things? Most were things I couldn't do anything about — things in the past. Some in the present I couldn't control, like whether it rained. I decided I'm too smart to waste so much effort needlessly."

Beware the Little Bugs

An old adage says, "It's not the great storm that destroys the giant oak tree — it's the little bugs!" It is ironic that we weather the great storms and crises in life and then allow insignificant, trifling irritations to destroy our happiness and health.

"We were acting pretty dumb about this a while back. We'd decide to go out for dinner, for fun and relaxation.

There we'd be in the car, dressed and ready to go. He'd say, 'Where shall we eat?' and I'd say, 'It doesn't matter,' and things would go downhill from there. I couldn't figure out why he was so hostile when I was just trying to be agreeable, and he couldn't understand why I was making him guess what I wanted.

"We have a very sound marriage, but this trifle almost got out of control. Soon it carried over into other conversations like 'Which movie shall we see?' 'Where shall we vacation?' Every decision ended in a fight.

"After one especially angry blowup, we had a long talk and discovered it was all a dumb misunderstanding. 'It doesn't matter' was my way of trying to be agreeable, but he resented having to make another decision. He makes decisions all day at work. So now I make a suggestion when he asks where or what. Sometimes I'll plan the evening and say, 'Come on. We're going out and it's a surprise.' I pick the restaurant and maybe plan a play or movie after. He enjoys the surprise and not having to choose."

Other strong family members agree that petty irritants should be recognized as petty. If at all possible just ignore some of them — the thoughtless action or word, the apparent insult. Children who leave dirty rooms behind them aren't trying to be mean to their parents; they're just being normal children. The neighbor who doesn't return your wave may not have seen you.

We asked, "What about the trivialities that can't be ignored? What about slurping coffee or mannerisms that drive you crazy or something that really hurts your feelings?" Our strong families gave sensible advice:

"Iron it out as soon as possible. Be nice. Say 'It really drives me nuts when you crack your knuckles. I know it isn't a big thing; you're a fine person with few flaws.' You'll both have a laugh and clear it up."

* *

"Don't let resentment build up. Don't pile misunderstanding and hurt on top of misunderstanding and hurt. Get it out in the open. Ask the person who hurt your feelings what was meant. You may discover you misinterpreted the action or words. If not, forgive them and go on to other things. Life is too short."

Refresh and Restore

A very few exceptional people seem to be able to go at a breakneck pace over a long period of time. These are folks who thoroughly enjoy their work. Consequently their work is like play to them; it *does* refresh them. Most of us are not so fortunate. Too much work, worry, stress, hassle, and confusion, and we succumb to burnout.

We all need to restore our minds, souls, and bodies. Our strong families do this largely through periodically participating in activities that are pleasant and relaxing.

"We like to take what we call 'aimless' trips about twice a year. We decide on a general destination not too far away. Then we set out and go as we please. We take state and county roads and drive leisurely. We explore little museums, quaint shops, and roadside markets. We stop early to enjoy a swim at the motel and a leisurely dinner."

* *

"Needlework is my refreshment. Nothing helps to take the tension away for me like an evening of knitting or crocheting."

* *

"We square dance one night a week. The kids have a junior square dance group in the same building."

* *

"I retreat to my workbench when I need to relax. I can absorb myself in some woodworking project for a couple of hours and then face the world again."

Get Outside

Strong families have a common characteristic of frequent participation in nature and outdoor activities together. Their outdoor pursuits include going on walks; camping; bird-watching; going on picnics; visiting zoos; parks, and nature reserves; fishing; and playing outdoor games together.

The strong families believe that these outdoor practices are such a powerful antidote to stress that they deserve special consideration. Their comments tell us more:

"Being out in nature puts life back in perspective for us. Go out on a clear night and look at the countless stars, and you'll know what is and isn't important. Observe the steady change of the seasons, and you'll know things take time so don't rush."

* *

"One of the real benefits of being out is being away from telephone, television, stereo, and other distractions. We can concentrate on each other. There's time to listen, to plan, to comfort, to dream."

* *

"Try hiking or backpacking or sailing or biking all day and feel that 'good' tired feeling of physical fatigue. So much of our fatigue these days is mental that it actually refreshes us to tire the body and let the mind rest."

Exercise

One of the most powerful neutralizers of stress is exercise. For years the world's most famous psychiatric and mental health clinics have prescribed up to fully half of the scheduled time each day for patients to be devoted to exercise and physical activities. Psychiatrists and counselors are well aware that exercise helps us to release our tension and get rid of pent-up frustration. The fatigue produced by exercise is, without a doubt, the best and the safest tranquilizer.[2]

Large numbers of strong families indicate they regularly participate in some form of exercise. The families are varied in terms of general health, age, and interests, so the specific forms of exercise vary as well. Bicycling, walking, golf, tennis, canoeing, swimming, skiing, jogging, and working out at a spa were all mentioned.

One executive summed up the benefit of exercise when he said,

"I get rid of lots of tension when I work out with weights. Something about tensing the muscles to lift or push makes the emotional tension release. Plus I feel stronger physically and better about myself, so naturally I am uplifted emotionally, too."

Minimize Fragmentation

Consider the following true story. The editor of one of the largest newspapers in the nation was very successful in his career. Active in community programs and various philanthropic endeavors, he practically never had an evening at home. He was always involved in a meeting or project. All of his projects were worthy, but all of them together were simply too much. A sad thing happened. He caught the flu, and his body's resistance was low from overwork and fragmentation. He died.

People literally can die from too much fragmentation, and so can families. Perhaps the most important thing we can do in dealing with the frantic pace of life is to reduce the number of our involvements. We can do what the strong families in our research practiced. You recall that repeatedly they told us they dealt with the hectic pace of life by scratching some activities off their lists, by clearing their calendars, by learning to say "no."

Another way strong families deal with the stress of too much to do and too many demands is to set priorities and simplify. Sandra, from Kentucky, was in the process of re-working priorities and simplifying when we talked with her. She works at an office and had been rushing home at 5:30 to prepare an elaborate dinner for her husband and teenage sons. After dinner she would do dishes and laundry and tidy the house. She also would scream at the boys a lot and have headaches and muscle spasms. Sandra began to make some changes. She decided dinner could be simpler — soup or something in the Crock Pot that would be ready when she got home. She found that teens can cook simple meals, too, and enjoy helping. They also can be responsible for their own laundry. Dishwashing and housecleaning chores were being shared. By deciding that her sanity was a higher prior-ity than doing everything for her family and by simplifying the menu and chores, Sandra is practicing good stress man-agement.

Pets

Bruce Max Feldmann, a prominent veterinary educator, has observed that pets are unique therapists and help mil-lions of people to cope better with life. They contribute to our emotional well-being, allowing us to love and feel love.[3]

Members of strong families mentioned the unconditional love and affection given by pets — especially dogs and cats — as a source of comfort. One Arkansas man said, "I take my old dog out to the creek when I feel sad or stretched too thin. We have a long walk and find a log or rock to sit down and have a talk. I can rant and rave and he listens. Pure love shines in his eyes."

A Connecticut woman talked about her cat:

"This cat of mine never sleeps on the bed with me. She prefers a chair in the dining room. Unless I am sick, and then she comes and sleeps on my feet. Don't ask me how she knows I have a cold or the flu; I guess it's a sixth sense. She acts like she's there to comfort me the only way she can."

Something Bigger than Self

Having a mission, goal, or being caught up in something larger than ourselves gives us security, confidence, and serenity to deal with the stresses of our daily lives. This was demonstrated so well by our strong families. The sense of purpose expressed among strong families revolved around their spiritual beliefs and their concern for each other.

One Wisconsin father confided a special insight to us:

"Sometimes in the scrambled schedule of life I get to feeling like the time I spend with my sons could better be spent on work. And then I remind myself that the budget request or schedule of who works when or the productivity report will affect life for a few days or weeks. I have to do it and it is somewhat important, but my job as a father is most important. If I'm a good father to my sons, they're likely to be good parents, too. Someday — after I'm gone, and certainly after those reports have rotted — a grandchild or great-grandchild of mine will have a good father because I was a good father. It's kind of a chain reaction."

A member of another strong family told us:

"The secret to not being overwhelmed is to be able to see the daily challenges and frustrations as contributing to something larger. Keep the big picture in mind. See those PTA meetings as improving the school; see your volunteer hours as easing someone's misery; see the work of caring for your family as creating healthy, productive people who'll make the world a better place."

YOU CAN'T HIDE, SO . . .

Paul Harvey often points out on his news broadcasts that "you can run but you can't hide." Some things are inescapable. The strain of daily life brings deadlines, pressures, irritations, frustrations, demands, hurts. Living brings change: a new baby, a new job, moving to another house or town, a divorce, a wedding, a promotion, children who are grown, retirement. And at some times life brings crises: illness, death, unemployment, fire, flood, earthquake, marital infidelity, bankruptcy.

Experts in stress management tell us that we are wrong to view stress as all bad. After all, a certain amount of tension may improve our performance on many tasks. Everyone has watched a favorite, highly favored football team be upset by a less talented team largely because they were "flat" — no emotion, no tension, no excitement.

We also are told that the Chinese symbol for the word *crisis* has two meanings: it stands for both "danger" and "opportunity." A look in the dictionary may surprise you. The word *crisis* does not necessarily have a negative connotation. It is seen simply as a "turning point."

The strong families we have studied have learned to manage the level of stress in their everyday lives. They can't eliminate it any more than you can, but they don't deplete their reserves of energy and emotion. When the major mishaps occur they have resources to call up. Like the Chinese confronted by "danger" they can look for "opportunity." And so strong families successfully cope with stress and crises.

PUTTING IT TO WORK

1. Find out how much stress is on you. Dr. Thomas Holmes, a psychiatrist at the University of Washington in Seattle, has developed the Social Readjustment Rating Scale. This test assigns point values for various stressors. To take the test, simply circle all the life changes you have experienced in the past year. Then add up the total of all the items that you circled.

If you score below 150 points, your stress level isn't very high. You probably aren't experiencing discomfort. If you scored between 150 and 300 points, you need to be careful to safeguard your health and make an effort to reduce stress. If you scored more than 300, you need to be especially careful and reduce stress.[4]

The Social Readjustment Rating Scale

Event	Impact*
1. Death of spouse	100
2. Divorce	73
3. Marital separation	65
4. Jail term	63
5. Death of close family member	63
6. Personal injury or loss	53
7. Marriage	50
8. Fired at work/lost job	47
9. Marital reconciliation	45
10. Retirement	45
11. Change in health of family member	44
12. Pregnancy	40
13. Sex difficulties	39
14. Gain of new family member	39
15. Business readjustment	39
16. Change in financial state	38
17. Death of a close friend	37
18. Change to different line of work	36
19. Change in number of arguments with spouse	35
20. Mortgage over $50,000[†]	31
21. Foreclosure of mortgage or loan	30
22. Change in responsibilities at work	29
23. Son or daughter leaving home	29
24. Trouble with in-laws	29
25. Outstanding personal achievement	28
26. Spouse begins or stops work	26
27. Begin or end school	26

Event	Impact*
28. Change in living conditions	25
29. Revision of personal habits	24
30. Trouble with boss	23
31. Change in work hours or conditions	20
32. Change in a residence	20
33. Change in schools	20
34. Change in recreation	20
35. Change in church activities	19
36. Change in social activities	19
37. Mortgage or loan less than $50,000[†]	17
38. Change in sleeping habits	16
39. Change in number of family get-togethers	15
40. Change in eating habits	15
41. Vacation	12
42. Christmas	12
43. Minor violations of the law	11

*Please remember that these are relative estimates of how stressful a life change usually is. Your circumstances may make any event more (or less) stressful for you. If, for example, both you and your spouse *must work full-time* to meet house and car payments, "fired at work" might need to be weighted a 75 rather than a 47 and "pregnancy" under these circumstances might more nearly be a 65 than a 40.

[†]Holmes's original figure was $10,000. We have inflated the figure (10 percent per year) to make it more realistic. And you may find it a more helpful estimate of the impact of financial stress to consider your total indebtedness. If, for example, you have an $80,000 home loan, a $15,000 loan for your two autos, and $10,000 in smaller loans (furniture, braces for the kids' teeth, college tuition, etc.), your total debt would be $115,000. You might want to give yourself credit for two $50,000 loans; give yourself 62 points (2 × 31) for impact.

2. Stress management workshops are offered by hospitals, businesses, the YMCA and YWCA, and community colleges. Find one that fits your schedule and budget.

3. Commit yourself to an exercise program. Walking generally does not cause physical damage, is effective, and FREE. Choose another kind of exercise if you prefer. You

might like to walk or jog three times each week by yourself and play tennis or bicycle with a loved one on Saturdays.

4. Cultivate your sense of humor. Collect Ogden Nash's poems or Erma Bombeck's books. Make a scrapbook of cartoons you especially enjoy. Buy a Garfield calendar. Use a videotape recorder to make a collection of your favorite comedy series — M*A*S*H or I Love Lucy reruns.

5. Find a hobby that refreshes and pleases you. Many people find it helpful to make their recreation something that contrasts with what they do all day. For example, if you read a good deal in your work, select a hobby that is manual — gardening or macramé. If you work with people all day, you might enjoy a solitary activity for fun. If your work is behind a desk, pick a hobby that is physically active.

6. Many husbands and wives have found it helpful to make (and to review periodically) plans concerning their deaths. They consult a lawyer about wills and keep them current. Each knows the other's wishes with regard to funerals or memorial services, burial, et cetera. Maybe more important, each knows the location of insurance policies, bank accounts, deeds to property, car titles, and other important papers. Children should be included in these discussions when they are older.

Make this review every few years (say, when you are twenty-five, thirty, thirty-five, et cetera, to help you remember). Celebrate with a nice dinner afterward. Planning like this *doesn't* make you die any sooner; it does help your family when the time comes.

7. Use television as a catalyst for discussions with your family. Consider the crises portrayed in television dramas. Ask your family: What can this person (family) do? What good can you see in this situation? Who could help? What did this person (family) do that helped? Hindered?

8. Discuss some hypothetical situations with the family. What would we do if:

the house burned?
we had a tornado, flood, or earthquake?
Dad (Mom) were seriously ill or died?
Grandma (Grandpa) had to come live with us?
we had to move to another town?

Young children may be frightened by such discussions, so use your judgment about including them. Usually, though, they will follow the emotional lead of their parents. If Mom and Dad can handle the discussion, they can.

8

Circle of Power

———◆———

Our long-time friend Dr. James Montgomery has served as director of the Gerontology Center at the University of Georgia for many years. He has said: "The emerging family of today has strength. We are discovering that love is all about us."[1]

We like Jim Montgomery's expression "love is all about us." People who live in strong families might sum up their feelings that way. The characteristics of strong families — their commitment, communication, time together, spiritual wellness, ability to cope with stress and crises, and expression of appreciation — interact, connect, and reinforce each other to form a net of strength all around them.

That's one of the wonderful things about the six characteristics of strong families; they aren't isolated. We examined each characteristic separately for the sake of simplicity, but they interact in complex ways.

Here are some examples. Commitment seems to underlie

many of the other qualities: the man who isn't *committed* to his family isn't likely to give much *time* and may not feel the need to pull together with them in a *crisis* or to improve *communication*. Families that spend *time* together reinforce *commitment* and *communication*. Expressed *appreciation* reinforces *commitment*. Good *communication* is necessary in *crises* and in expressing *appreciation*. *Spiritual wellness* is central to *coping in crises, appreciating* the value of people, valuing *time together,* and in being *committed* to each other.

You might picture the characteristics as we have drawn them below.

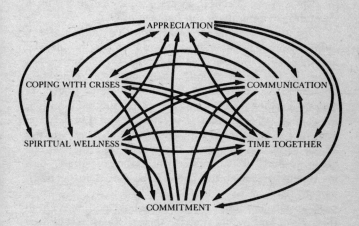

It gives a general indication of the interactions we talked about. Ignore the specifics of the interactions; ignore the crossed lines and tangled arrows. Look at the figure as a whole, and you see a circle — a circle of power — a circle of power that families may tap. Imagine yourself at the center of this circle. You can quickly see how strong families can energize and strengthen individual members.

CAN THE WEAK BECOME STRONG?

"Look," a distressed woman confronted us not long ago, "what your research shows about strong families is all well and fine. But my family is a real mess. We bring out the worst in each other; we're plagued with problems. I don't think there is hope for us. Can weak families become strong?"

We answered her question with two questions: Can people change? Can you learn different ways of relating to others?

The answers, of course, are *yes!* People change and learn every day, so naturally it can happen for you.

One thing causing problems for this woman was a faulty — although common — assumption that people who are successful have always been that way. We're surprised to learn that Woody Allen, successful writer/producer/director/actor, flunked motion picture production at New York University, and Leon Uris, successful author, failed high school English *three* times, and Liv Ullman, successful actress, failed an audition for the state theater school in Norway because the judges said she had no talent, and Albert Einstein, Nobel Laureate, didn't pass his college entrance exams.[2] And the list could be much longer.

So, too, successful, strong families have not always been that way. Many would describe themselves as having been weak, mediocre, or at the verge of breaking up; many have overcome communication problems, infidelity, lack of interest, outside demands, alcohol or drug abuse, or family violence to become the strong families they are today. Please remember the word *become*.

Ellen, a West Virginia woman, told her family's story.

"There was a time when our family was not strong. My husband and I had drifted away from each other. We didn't communicate. We had serious financial problems. Because we were head over heels in debt my husband, Carl, and I began to moonlight with second jobs.

"Unfortunately, we took our frustrations out on each other and the kids. We had terrible arguments over trivial things. One night one of these arguments ended with my husband hitting me hard in the face. He was very apologetic and genuinely sorry for what happened. Three weeks later, however, the same thing happened, only this time he hit me repeatedly. I was hurt so badly I had to go to the hospital. My nose was broken and my jaw was dislocated. I remember lying in that hospital bed thinking that it was all over. There was nothing left to hold our family together.

"I refused to see Carl or take his calls. He sent several notes, which I threw away unopened. I decided divorce was the only answer.

"The divorce proceedings progressed over the next several weeks. Strangely, I didn't feel any sense of relief or satisfaction; I felt empty. One day, my Aunt Helen, who has always been particularly close to me, said, 'What's wrong, Ellen? You look as though you are in another world.'

" 'It doesn't feel right, Aunt Helen,' I replied. 'I thought the divorce would be best for everybody. But now, I'm not sure. The children aren't happy. I'm certainly not happy. And Carl . . .'

" 'Do you feel there is anything in your marriage worth saving?' my aunt asked.

"I could not reply.

" 'If you want to save your marriage you cannot dwell on the past,' Aunt Helen said. 'If you and Carl give it everything you have, maybe you can build your family into what you want it to be.'

" 'But our family has been such a terrible failure,' I replied.

" 'You can learn from your failures' was Aunt Helen's response. 'You don't have to remain in them. Learning from your mistakes can help you succeed in the future. They can be your guides for what to avoid and what to do differently tomorrow.'

"My aunt's words echoed in my thoughts for a long time. I decided one thing — we had not given our marriage and family everything we had. I certainly had not. Both Carl and I were guilty of extreme neglect of our marriage and family. What would happen if we really did commit ourselves to each other and the kids?

"You see what we had really been committed to, what we focused our time and attention on to that point, was work — two jobs each — and making ends meet. And yes we were also committed to our misery. We spent a lot of time being frustrated, mad, and hassled. Because there was not time for anything else, we just left each other out. I think we unconsciously knew what was happening but didn't know how to change it. That may be why the arguments became so violent.

"I picked up the phone and called Carl and said I thought we should get together and talk. We did. We had several talks over the next two weeks. We talked more openly and honestly than we had done at any time in our marriage. We even cried together, particularly in the first meeting. Carl told me that he had joined a group for abusive men and had been going to their meetings for several weeks. He was so ashamed and shocked that he had lost control like that.

"I told him that we had all lost control of our lives. At the suggestion of our minister, who is also a certified family therapist, we made a list of what had been wrong in our marriage and what we wanted to change. We set goals for what we wanted our family to become. And then we developed realistic plans to accomplish those goals.

"One of the first things we did was to quit our second jobs. They were creating too much stress and did not leave us any time for each other. We cut our expenses by selling one of our two cars. That eliminated one expensive monthly payment. We also moved into a smaller house. We don't eat out very often; I sew my own clothes; we don't have any expensive hobbies. It wasn't easy, but we started making ends meet financially.

"Another goal of ours was to spend a lot more time together as a family. And we wanted it to be pleasant — fun — recreational. It was something of a shock to us when we realized that in the past we had been doing nothing together that was fun or enjoyable. What little time we had spent together was simply tired, irritable people going through the motions of surviving day to day. No wonder our family had not been a happy place to live. Maybe our violent arguments had been a cry for help — a way of saying something has to change.

"I expressed concern to our minister as to whether it was possible for us to change. 'To make a go of it as a family we have to make some big changes. I don't know if it's realistic. Can we really do it?'

"His answer was 'Do you want to do it?' I said, 'Yes, more than anything else.'

" 'Good. You're more than halfway there,' he said. 'Continue making your action plans for a successful, happy family. Now I think there is only one other thing you need.'

" 'What is that?' I asked.

" 'To realize that you are not in this alone,' he replied. 'You have each other and some of your relatives and friends. And do you believe God helps people?'

" 'Yes,' I answered.

" 'Then remember you have a group of people cheering you on and hoping for the best for you. Think of them as resources and as your cheerleading section,' he responded.

"We began family prayers each evening before dinner. Not just a blessing for the meal. We prayed for ourselves and our family and for other people as well.

"Well, the changes came — slowly, but they came. And

they were good changes. We began to spend a lot more time together. We made sure at least two nights each week were fun nights where the whole family did enjoyable activities together like playing cards or board games.

"Because we were spending more time with our children, we came to know them in a way we never had before. Carl and I truly discovered each other for the first time. We found we genuinely like each other. We spend a lot of time talking and listening to each other. Our sex life is much better, too.

"We all became kinder and more supportive in our relationships. We concentrated on making each other feel good about ourselves rather than tearing each other down and constantly criticizing and fussing at each other.

"That turning point for us was years ago. We still have quarrels but I'm glad to say they aren't violent anymore. Over time our family has evolved into a happy place to be. We came from a long way back to become a strong family. It was more than worth the effort!"

BECOMING

Remember we asked you to keep that word in mind? Strong families don't spring forth full-blown each time the moon is full. No secret incantation will do the trick. Lots of effort and cooperation will.

And the effort to become a stronger family is ongoing. The strong families we talked with told us that they continue to work on their relationships, they continue to cherish and nourish the family.

We have included two checklists and a Family Strength Inventory in the "Putting It to Work" section at the conclusion of this chapter. We mention them here because we feel they are useful tools for looking at your family situation. They will give you some idea of where your strengths and weaknesses are; they can get you and your family started on becoming stronger.

Do It Yourself

Becoming a stronger, happier, healthier, more successful family will begin with your family. You and your spouse and children (or some combination of those) will be the ones who decide to make the changes, adjustments, and improvements that will make better communication, create a more pleasant environment, reduce stress, allow more time together, and nurture specific values. Probably 95 percent or more of the effort and problem solving will come exclusively from your family. Becoming a stronger family is definitely a do-it-yourself project. That's fine; it works well for most families.

With a Little Help from Friends

You need not struggle through alone. Sometimes we need an instruction book or a demonstration to get us started on the right foot in our do-it-yourself projects. Fortunately, there are aids for families interested in becoming stronger.

We hope this book has been helpful. We can't think of anyone better to ask for advice than the strong families all around us. They're real experts on how to make strong families.

Other books are available at bookstores and public libraries. You can find many with information about communication; managing finances; parenting; sexuality; building self-esteem; managing stress; coping with divorce, death, unemployment, and illness; and increasing spirituality.

Marriage and Family Enrichment

We also suggest that you consider taking a course in marriage enhancement, personal wellness, surviving dual careers, parenting, managing stress, or whatever might be offered by your community college, YMCA, YWCA, or churches in your community. Many offer excellent classes at reasonable costs; some provide child care while you attend class. Courses of this kind are a relaxed way to learn methods to improve your family while you enjoy the company of persons with similar interests and situations.

One of the most exciting developments in the field of family studies in the past decade or so has been the explosion of interest in prevention and enhancement. The field of marriage and family enrichment is growing by leaps and bounds, as people are discovering the benefits of enhancing a basically sound marriage, rather than trying to find a miracle cure for a terminally ill relationship.

Hundreds of marriage enrichment programs can be found around the country. Look around and you'll likely find one that suits your philosophy, values, and style because there are many approaches to marriage and family enrichment. Some, like "Marriage Encounter," have a religious flavor because they come out of churches or synagogues. Others do not because they are offered by community mental health centers, schools, universities, or family service agencies.

The format of marriage and family enrichment programs varies as well. You'll find discussions, readings, lectures, films, homework, and combinations of these techniques.

What else can you expect from marriage enrichment? Expect a pleasant association with other couples — some of them absolutely fascinating — interested in improving their marriages. Expect some fun and laughs and some work. Be prepared for the discovery that your problems aren't all that unique. We call this the "gee whiz" phenomenon. It happens when the light bulbs go on in people's minds and they say (or think): "Gee whiz, you mean you have trouble [pick one or more] talking with your wife about sex, getting your kids to listen to you, feeling good about being 'just a housewife,' balancing all the bills on a teacher's paycheck, feeling positive about your father-in-law? et cetera. You know, I have trouble with that, too!"

Expect your marriage — if it is basically sound — to improve, but don't expect *drastic* changes. Most enrichment programs last six to ten weeks and that's not time enough for drastic changes. To increase their value, many marriage enrichment programs encourage couples to continue to meet on their own after the official meetings have concluded. Typically, the couples meet for a potluck dinner and conversation on a monthly basis. Sometimes close friendships develop.

Don't expect marriage enrichment to patch together a seriously troubled marriage. The aim of these programs is *enrichment,* not counseling. The leader of the marriage enrichment experience privately may suggest family therapy for a couple who seem to have very serious difficulties.

Marriage and Family Therapy

That brings us to our final suggestion: namely, that a marriage and family therapist can be real help for some situations. We realize some of you turned pale or blushed at that suggestion. There is still the incorrect notion that only "crazy" people go to a counselor or therapist. We'd like to turn that around: sometimes people are "crazy" *not* to go for help. Think about it: you aren't ashamed to haul your car to a mechanic when it makes strange noises, and you call a plumber when the tub refuses to drain, and you let an electrician handle your wiring problems. We don't expect to fill our own teeth, build our own homes, or fly our own airplanes. We depend on professionals there.

Family relationship problems aren't really so different. If you haven't learned good communication skills or other relationship skills (just like people learn plumbing skills!) you may benefit from outside help from a professional.

It is difficult to establish a rule of thumb concerning how you know if you need to visit a family therapist. Some symptoms that tend to indicate a need for a therapist's help would include spouse abuse, either physical or mental; child abuse or neglect; alcohol or drug abuse; serious dissatisfaction with the relationship; ongoing depression; an extramarital affair; children having lots of trouble at school or getting into trouble (vandalism, thefts, fights, et cetera); spouse completely withdrawn, uninterested, noncommunicative; and serious consideration of divorce. If you're in doubt, we suggest you visit a therapist. One or two visits will help you decide if you want more.

How do you pick a good marriage and family therapist? Begin by looking at the person's professional qualifications. The counselor should be willing to discuss his or her background and training with you. Marriage and family counselors come from a number of different backgrounds. Some were trained specifically for marriage and family counseling in a university or training center; others come from the more general professions of psychology, social work, family studies, psychiatry, or the ministry, to name a few. Some counselors are certified by the American Association of Marriage and Family Therapists (AAMFT). This means they have done extensive counseling under the supervision of an experienced therapist.

We also suggest you ask prospective counselors about their approach or their philosophies of treatment. Some counselors use a family systems approach, others are behavioral therapists, others emphasize reality therapy or do nondirective counseling. Most use a combination of techniques and strategies. Each should be able to explain his or her approach in a way that you can understand. Be sure the approach makes sense to you personally.

Personal characteristics of counselors also vary widely. We tend to lean toward counselors who are kind, rational, honest, open, forgiving, humble, and humorous. Other people are very happy with counselors who may possess very different qualities. Again, it's an individual matter.

If you know someone who has visited a therapist, ask him

or her for recommendations. Like everything else: shop around.

You may wish to inquire about the counselor's fees. These vary. Some counselors and counseling agencies charge on a sliding fee scale based upon income. A single parent we know recently went for professional help because of the stress and loneliness of her divorce. The agency, on the basis of the woman's low income, charged her only $1.75 per session. "And I get a ten percent discount for paying the day of the session!" she laughed.

Generally, a counselor's fee will run from $25 to $75 or more per session. Cost alone is not an accurate measure of how good a counselor is, so weigh other factors in making your choice.

Successful counseling may take several sessions. We believe along with a lot of other counselors that a minimum of six or eight would be fairer to the counselor and the marriage; if significant progress can't be made in that time, other arrangements should be made.

And, if significant progress is being made, and everyone included feels good about the process, a family could justifiably stay with a counselor for a long time: weekly, or bi-weekly, or monthly for a year or more. It depends upon the goals the family has set and how difficult and time-consuming these goals are to achieve.

REACHING OUT TO OTHER FAMILIES

So far we have focused on what people in strong families do to enhance family development and what the family can do to improve itself. But in our contact with people from strong families it was also quite clear that their love for each other was very often complemented by a love for other people in other families in their community.

Strong family members have a commitment to a spiritual dimension of life, a life of principled service to God or humankind or some higher good. This is reflected in their behavior toward people outside the family as well as inside the family.

Service to other families in the community takes many forms — on an individual basis and through membership in various organizations and agencies. One experienced older mother of three who knows only too well how difficult and frustrating children can be tells us that whenever she goes shopping she usually witnesses one or two harried and younger mothers trying to buy groceries. Their babies and toddlers are invariably wailing and running amok in the aisles, causing the young mothers anxiety and embarrassment. "Why are my kids so awful?" the young parent's face seems to be saying. She may be about to pinch or spank or slap the child.

The mother talking with us has a kind way of helping. She goes up and talks gently with the mother: "I've got three kids. Whew! It's sure hard. Can I hold her while you shop? I'll keep her busy with a cracker . . . ," et cetera.

In this way she calms the waters and saves a child from further pain and a frustrated parent from feelings of guilt and inadequacy.

With people we know from a synagogue or church or work or as neighbors, it's even easier to be supportive. We can sense when another person is upset, and rather than ignore him or her or walk away thinking misery is better left alone, we can become involved. This can mean simply listening and caring as they tell their tales of woe.

"I feel so stupid," Ed told his friend. "I haven't had a job for five months. I just can't find one." Ed's friend had heard him yelling in frustration one morning and went next door to see what was wrong. Ed had been roaring with the full force his lungs could muster, and the bathroom cabinet and walls almost shook. His neighbor Arlan chose to get involved.

Arlan helped Ed get the brakes and clutch fixed in Ed's car and he called five friends to see if they knew of work.

Ed doesn't have a job yet, but he doesn't feel totally alone in an uncaring world. "You kept me from running away from it all," he admitted to Arlan a bit sheepishly. "I was about to leave Nancy and the kids and run. I just couldn't stand it anymore."

With Arlan and a handful of other friends around to offer help in simple, practical ways, Ed probably *will* make it.

Members of strong families told us about their involvement in the lives of other families. A few of the ways they help are by the following:

coaching a soccer or baseball team for their kids and a bunch of other people's kids;

volunteering to lead the community choir;

taking the Girl Scout troop on a bicycle tour ("That was the greatest experience of my life," one girl told the leader, Mrs. Jamison, five years later);

helping a friend fix his roof, thus taking financial pressure off him;

taking food to the parents whose baby died and staying for several hours to eat the food, as it turns out, and to cry with them over the loss;

offering to have some friends' teenager stay over while they go on vacation for two weeks ("Oh, come on, Dad! I'm sick of my sisters. Why can't I stay with Mr. and Mrs. Smith? Huh?");

serving as captain of the Neighborhood Watch crime-prevention program and taking the time to chat with the older, isolated persons on the rounds to distribute literature.

The list is potentially endless. We support the development of strong families in our community each time we serve families in a way that brings joy and self-esteem to them.

And we are repaid tenfold in satisfaction and joy brought to our own lives.

Even when people are in the midst of a crisis, we as counselors like to recommend they continue to serve others. It helps them get their minds off of troubles that can drown them and it brings satisfaction that, even in the depths of despair, we can as human beings find goodness in our world.

WHAT CAN SOCIETY DO FOR FAMILIES?

Besides those working as individuals in their communities to build family strengths, there are many other concerned citizens who have chosen to get involved from a different perspective. These folks want to work through government and the political process to bring about change.

Which is the better route to go? Get involved in a campaign to write a new law or develop a new program? Or teach the preschoolers on your block the fun of making sand castles?

Pick either task you like; neither is *better*. Both approaches have an important place in life. Some of us are better working in our neighborhoods. Some have a gift for public speaking or writing, and the fortitude to try to move society. We need people of all kinds working together in countless ways to build family strengths.

The future of families in this country will be decided in great measure by what we as a society do to enhance family potential. Individual families do not live in a vacuum. For families that wish to develop their potential, the task is made much more difficult in a world torn by war or if they are threatened by racism, sexism, ageism, unemployment, environmental degradation — a host of massive societal and international problems.

The reader may think we are about to mount some kind of political soapbox. But we aren't.

First of all, that wouldn't work because Nick and John are different in many ways in their politics. They don't talk about whom they vote for because they get along better by ignoring the subject and, more important, the task of building family strengths transcends mere politics. It is much more important than which team you choose to play on. It is more important than all the hoopla of the political game.

Let us tell you what 2,000 delegates to the recently held White House Conference on Families did when they managed to put politics aside and talk about what we as a society need to do to enhance family life. Their twenty top recommendations are terrific in our estimation, and we encourage you to get involved in any number of ways to help implement these recommendations.

The delegates to the conference came from every U.S. state and territory. They came from every walk of life. Nearly 1,600 were chosen at the state level; 310 were appointed as delegates-at-large; 55 were state coordinators; and 40 were members of the White House Conference on Families Advisory Committee.

The delegates met in Minneapolis, Baltimore, and Los Angeles. In less than three days they waded through a mountain of raw material — seven national hearings, 5,000 state recommendations, the recommendations of many national organizations, Gallup survey results, and their own experience and expertise. The recommendations moved through three groups of delegate work groups of 30 to 40 persons, topic sessions of 125 to 175 persons, and plenary meetings of the entire Conference. The Conference was a massive undertaking and the delegates' recommendations are worth looking at seriously:

1. A call for family-oriented personnel policies — flextime, leave policies, shared and part-time jobs, transfer policies (92 percent of the 2,000 delegates voted yes on this recommendation).

2. New efforts to prevent alcohol and drug abuse — education and media initiatives (92.7 percent voted yes).

3. Major changes in the tax code to eliminate the marriage tax penalty, revise inheritance taxes, and recognize homemakers (92.1 percent).

4. Tax policies to encourage home care of aging and handicapped persons (92.0 percent).

5. Greater assistance to families with a handicapped member — tax credits, financial help, et cetera (91.0 percent).

6. A call for a systematic analysis of all laws, regulations, and rules for their impact on families (90.4 percent).

7. Efforts to increase public awareness and sensitivity toward persons with handicapping conditions (90.1 percent).

8. Government efforts to assist handicapped persons — enforce existing laws, et cetera (89.8 percent).

9. Encourage independence and home care for aging persons — tax incentives, housing programs (89.0 percent).

10. More equitable economic treatment of full-time homemakers — social security changes, programs for displaced homemakers (87.4 percent).

11. Reform of social security — eliminate biases against families, marriage, homemakers (84.9 percent).

12. Increased pressure on media to curb excess violence, sex stereotypes (83.4 percent).

13. Increased efforts to combat employment discrimination (83.0 percent).

14. Support for family-violence prevention efforts and services (82.0 percent).

15. Involvement of families in improved family support services and self-help efforts (81.5 percent).

16. Support for full employment (81.4 percent).

17. Development of coherent energy and inflation policies (79.4 percent).

18. Promotion of and support for a variety of childcar

choices — home, community, and center-based care and parental choice (79.0 percent).

19. Improved tax incentives for family housing (78.3 percent).

20. Increased efforts to prevent and deal with adolescent pregnancy (77.9 percent).[3]

Many observers were surprised by the behavior of the delegates to the White House Conference on Families. It had been predicted that the conference would bog down in endless squabbles over highly emotional issues such as abortion, divorce, feminism, welfare, and day care. But there was a surprising degree of broad agreement on a wide range of proposals. In summary, three-fourths of the delegates agreed on three-fourths of the recommendations. There is, indeed, a good degree of national consensus about what needs to be done to help families. This, we believe, holds exciting possibilities.

THE BEST INVESTMENT

We said at the beginning of this book that our story is not of gloom and doom and the ultimate demise of the family. We happen to think family is too important to us, as individuals, as nations, and as a world, to disappear. Family forms may change to meet our needs, but family goes on and on. We aren't alone in that idea. The family has been described as the nucleus of civilization and as the natural, fundamental unit of society.[4] And the thousands of strong families who told their secrets to us add their agreement. Family is vital and here to stay.

It follows logically, then, that we and the strong families we talked with believe the cost of becoming a strong family isn't too high. Effort, work, learning to say "I'm sorry," compromise, learning new skills, scratching other involvements off the list, devoting time to each other, learning to appreciate each other, and putting family as number one in our priorities do cost us. Becoming a strong family demands an investment of time, energy, spirit, and heart.

Dr. Joyce Brothers, noted psychologist, columnist, and author, wrote recently about one of her investments. This example speaks of the kinds of things strong families do to become stronger. Dr. Brothers and her husband, Milt, especially enjoy breakfast together; it is a special time for them. She continued:

> But I know Milt feels better about life when I'm there to make breakfast and eat it with him. And I feel better too.
>
> This is the reason I do not do extended lecture tours. It would make much more sense when I have a lecture date in Dallas, for instance, to accept engagements in Houston and Corpus Christi and Austin and spend four or five days at a time in Texas. But I don't. I do my lecture in Dallas and then I fly home. If I have a lecture in Houston the next day, I fly to Texas again. I often do the round trip between Los Angeles and New York three times a week just so I can be home at night and have breakfast with Milt in the morning.
>
> It can be exhausting, but I feel it is worth the extra effort.[5]

Ellen, from West Virginia, earlier in the chapter said, "It was more than worth the effort." Other strong family members have said the same: the effort is worth it; they don't regret their sacrifices for family.

One woman said, "I look at what I put into my family — my sweat and tears and love and muscle and mind — as an investment in their future, my future, our future. It's *the best* investment I can make."

THE BEGINNING

A man and his young son walked along the edge of the beach. They stopped and looked out at the endless ocean.

"Just think, Joey," said the father, "the waves that are now breaking at our feet have come from far across the sea."

After a few moments the father noticed the young boy had a sad look on his face. "What's wrong, Joey?" the father asked.

"The waves are dying at our feet," said Joey. "They come to the end of their long trip from across the ocean and then they die. This is the end for the waves."

"No," the father replied, "this is not the end. This is the beginning — the beginning of their long journey back across the sea."

Coming to the end of this book has been hard for us. Like Joey, we feel a little sad. From across the vast expanse of this great nation as well as other countries around the world, the strong families have sent us their wisdom and insight about building family strengths and encircling relationships. We thank them for their unselfish sharing.

And now we're tempted to keep adding more information. But we don't need to tell you more. You have a solid foundation from the strong families. You also have within you everything you need to create your own strong family.

This point of our relationship with you is much like the incoming tide. It seems like the end. But as Joey's father said, this is not the end. This is really the beginning of your quest for a stronger, happier family. Your quest can benefit not only you but the lives of your children and your children's children. There will be a ripple effect extending far into the future.

We wish you good luck!

PUTTING IT TO WORK

1. We like to invite panels of divorced persons to come to talk about their experiences to the marriage and family classes we teach. Students are stunned to hear about alcoholism or spouse abuse or infidelity. But the most sobering experience is hearing about a marriage and family that just burned out.

Marriage burnout comes on so slowly and quietly that the couple often aren't aware of it. Sometimes one spouse hides dissatisfactions for years before speaking of them; sometimes both try to ignore the warning signs.

The following checklist of symptoms of burnout can give you some ideas of potential problems in your marriage. The earlier you treat the symptoms the better your chances of a "cure." Expect to check some of the items; on the average, married persons check five to ten areas. The lowest ever checked was three and the highest was thirty-five.

Symptoms of Marriage "Burnout"

_____ loss of interest in each other

_____ lack of communication

_____ nothing in common

_____ don't do things together, or don't care to do things together, or can't find the time

_____ marriage is not the top priority anymore; job, church, relatives, friends, hobbies, lovers, whatever, are more important

_____ you're facing up to the fact that deep down you want a divorce

_____ inflexibility — you can no longer compromise with each other

_____ you feel you have an unequal share of the workload

_____ minor irritations become major issues (which are just a smokescreen for the underlying problem)

_____ failure to try to deal honestly with important issues

_____ you make family decisions alone

_____ you make assumptions about your spouse without talking with him or her

_____ you have more intimate relationships with other people than your spouse

_____ boredom

_____ you have differing values

_____ lack of romance, touching, cuddling

_____ job problems become paramount to everything else

_____ child-rearing philosophies differ

_____ the children start acting up; they have frequent trouble at school, get in fights with friends, or they withdraw

_____ one spouse controls the other by violence, tantrums, or threats of suicide or violence

_____ individual interests are more important than the welfare of the couple

_____ you can't talk about money, politics, religion, sex, or other touchy subjects

_____ nitpicking

_____ you avoid each other

_____ public humiliation

_____ you aren't concerned about how you look anymore, nor about how she or he looks, either

_____ health problems, such as headaches, back pain, sleeplessness, high blood pressure, recurring colds, emotional ups and downs

_____ alcohol and other drug abuse

_____ you feel like you've forfeited your own happiness for the well-being of the other person

_____ family functions decrease

_____ no one listens anymore

_____ one grows in one direction, one grows in the other direction

_____ your family goals are petty and meaningless, you are lost in the quest for money, success, or material possessions, and hunger for a more transcendent purpose in life

_____ you feel a need for involvement in some kind of spiritual or religious community, but your partner balks or cannot agree on a choice

_____ irritability

_____ withdrawal

_____ sarcasm

_____ you're staying in the relationship because it's easier than being on your own

_____ you don't have any disagreements or arguments anymore

We suggest that you and your spouse do the checklist separately and then compare answers. This isn't easy to do, by any means, but problems aren't apt to go away by themselves. Together you can probably clear them away.

2. The checklist that follows has a series of suggestions for enhancing family relationships. Read through the list, giving yourself (your family) a "+" for the ones you already do to an extent that satisfies you; give yourself a "0" for the ones you feel neutral or so-so about (you could do better but aren't completely unhappy about it); give yourself a "−" for the suggestions that are lacking in your family. Again, it is helpful to have each family member complete the checklist separately and then compare answers.

Enhancing Relationships Checklist

_____ Look for the good in each other instead of always focusing on the bad. Express this appreciation often (like every day or more often).

_____ Commit yourselves to your family; don't give up on it easily. Our families bring some of the most beautiful times in our lives and some of the most difficult; ride out the storms together.

_____ Act as if your family is more important than anything else — work, school, friends, relatives, church; don't pay lipservice to it, hypocritically.

_____ Be more open and honest in your communication without being negative; express your honest concerns without attacking.

_____ Eliminate violence in relationships. Learn to argue without using your fists. Find ways of disciplining children that do not require slapping or spanking (for example "Time Out": "Because you continue to pick on little sister, you must sit quietly on this chair for five minutes," or withdrawal of privileges: "If you don't quit yelling and running through the house, you'll not get to watch cartoons this afternoon").

_____ Work on problems when they arise, rather than letting them build up until a huge blowup is inevitable.

_____ Spend lots and lots of time together just enjoying each other's company; if you forgot how to enjoy each other's company, relearn this art just like you learned how to bowl or do needlepoint.

_____ Reinforce positive behaviors. Tell your husband how much you like his efforts to improve communication; accept compliments from your kids graciously and make them feel good in return.

_____ Build self-esteem and confidence. If you find yourself chewing out a loved one, you must find ten occasions to compliment him or her before you complain again. Remember how easily esteem buckets are emptied; how hard they are to fill.

_____ Discuss your values with your loved ones. What do you find important about life? What are you working toward and growing toward? What kinds of religious orientation does each of you hold and how can this be used to bolster your life together?

_____ Have a Marriage Annual Meeting. Leave town together and check into a motel. Write down beforehand how each of your lives as an individual is going, and how each of you thinks the family is going, and where you want to go as individuals and as a family together. Build direction for your lives together. Celebrate your accomplishments (ten years of marriage and two fine children, or whatever) and have some fun, too.

_____ Allow for the growth of each individual. Don't smother each other. But at the same time don't let *individuality* be a copout word which really means "I don't care anymore and I'm just not going to try — but I'll fake it."

_____ Compromise. The best solution is one in which no one wins and no one loses. Instead, make the relationship win.

_____ Find a cause or purpose in life that is bigger than you and your family — fight world hunger; work for peace or an end to birth defects or to reduce crime in your town; adopt a child; be active in your synagogue or church. Work as a family.

_____ You'd consider taking a class on macramé or income tax preparation or exercise, so why not one on marriage enrichment or parenting?

_____ Let a marriage and family therapist help with

especially troublesome areas. It takes maturity and foresight to deal with problems before they become a crisis.

_____ Develop individual responsibilities in the family, but remember that these will inevitably change with time. Be flexible and avoid sex stereotypes. If it makes more sense or satisfies the couple, there is no reason why he can't cook and iron while she mows the lawn or waxes the car.

_____ Treat your loved ones as kindly as you would a best friend or your boss. Loved ones are most important of all, and deserve the best.

_____ Children can add strength to a relationship and encourage commitment; but they also can slowly and steadily erode the relationship by taking so much energy and time away from it. Don't let being a parent stop you from being a spouse.

_____ Try heart-to-heart talks on a regular basis. Sit down with plenty of time (at least an hour), no phone, and a glass of apple cider or soda pop. Talk about what's happening in each of your lives. How does each of you feel? Where's the family going? Do this with the kids, too.

_____ How's your sex life? Seriously, most couples find that improving their relationship improves their sexual relationship. Sometimes it works, too, that improving sex improves the general relationship. A reputable book on human sexuality may be of help — or a weekend away from the kids or a new nightie or a shower together or flowers.

_____ Deal with stress on a daily basis. Exercise, relaxation, humor, perspective, hobbies, and pets are weapons in the fight against stress.

_____ Think about general actions you can take in the event of a crisis. Regard crises as opportunities to grow closer as a family.

Give your family a pat on the back for each + you accumulated. Look again at the 0's and −'s; they indicate areas of potential growth. Finally make a list of five areas you would like to work on, giving a number one to the most important, most urgent area.

3. The Family Strengths Inventory has been developed from the questionnaires used in our research projects. It is a shortened version. Directions for scoring follow the Inventory. Fill it out.

Family Strengths Inventory

Circle on a five-point scale (with 1 representing the least degree and 5 representing the greatest degree) the degree to which your family possesses each one of the following.

Spending time together and doing things with each other

1   2   3   4   5

Commitment to each other

1   2   3   4   5

Good communication (talking with each other often, listening well, sharing feelings with each other)

1   2   3   4   5

Dealing with crises in positive manner

1   2   3   4   5

Expressing appreciation to each other

1   2   3   4   5

Spiritual wellness

1   2   3   4   5

Circle the degree of closeness of your relationship with your spouse on a five-point scale (with 1 representing the least degree and 5 representing the greatest degree).

1   2   3   4   5

Circle the degree of closeness of your relationship with

your children on a five-point scale (with 1 representing the least degree and 5 representing the greatest degree).

1 2 3 4 5

Circle the degree of happiness of your relationship with your spouse on a five-point scale (with 1 representing the least degree and 5 representing the greatest degree).

1 2 3 4 5

Circle the degree of happiness of your relationship with your children on a five-point scale (with 1 representing the least degree and 5 representing the greatest degree).

1 2 3 4 5

Some people make us feel good about ourselves. That is, they make us feel self-confident, worthy, competent, and happy about ourselves. What is the degree to which your spouse makes you feel good about yourself? Indicate on the following five-point scale (with 1 representing the least degree and 5 representing the greatest degree).

1 2 3 4 5

Indicate on the following five-point scale the degree to which you think you make your spouse feel good about himself/herself (with 1 representing the least degree and 5 representing the greatest degree).

1 2 3 4 5

Indicate on the following five-point scale the degree to which you think you make your children feel good about themselves (with 1 representing the least degree and 5 representing the greatest degree).

1 2 3 4 5

To obtain your score on the Inventory, simply add the numbers you have circled. Your score will fall in a range between 13 and 65.

What does your score mean? A score below 39 represents a below-average score. Don't run off to your lawyers to file for divorce. You just have some work to do to improve your family life. Look back at the individual questions to target areas to begin working on. For example, if you circled a 5 on commitment but a 1 on spending time together, your family could benefit from some shared activities.

A score of 39 to 52 indicates an average score. Again, you can refer to individual questions to spot strengths and weaknesses. A score above 52 indicates a strong family. Remember that relationships need continued nurture, so don't use a high score as an excuse to become complacent.

4. A midwestern farmer's six-year-old daughter was looking at the seed soon to be planted. From the seed would grow hundreds of acres of wheat that would soon wave majestically in the wind. The daughter held the seed in her hand as she asked, "Daddy, will wheat really grow from this?"

When her father assured her it would, she replied, "I don't see how. It doesn't look anything like wheat."

Perhaps your family does not at the moment look anything like a strong family to you. But the seeds for growth are at your disposal. You can have a strong family. The success you hope for can be attained.

What do you want your family to become in the future? Visualize what you want to see happen in your family relationships. Decide on some goals.

Perhaps you want your family to have more fun times together. It may be important to everyone in your family that there be more time to simply sit down and talk with each other in a leisurely, relaxed manner.

Write these desires down on a piece of paper. In fact, get everyone in the family to identify what they would most like to see happen in the family. As a family, agree on the ten that are most important.

Look at the list. This is a part of your family potential. As the seed turns into the full-grown wheat, so your present family relationship may evolve into what you most desire for your family to become.

In order to move successfully toward your family potential you need a strong desire and commitment to those goals and an action plan. Call it a family potential action plan.

For example, you have decided that one of your goals is to have more fun time together as a family. Start by having the family identify several activities that everyone in the family enjoys. Then make sure the family participates in some of those activities on a weekly basis. Perhaps everyone enjoys board games. Then reserve two evenings a week for board games. Agree on a specific time you will begin this — then do it. (See the example below.)

It may be helpful for you as a family to establish a family potential action plan revolving around the six qualities characterizing our strong families. Give it a try. Your family potential action plan can be an important aid in helping your family potential to become reality. It can be a seed which facilitates the growth of your family strengths.

Family Potential Action Plan

Strong Family Quality	*What We Want to Happen (Our Goals)*	*How We Are Going to Do It (Our Strategies)*	*Specific Time We Will Start*
Commitment			
Appreciation			
Spending time together	more fun time as a family	reserve 2 evenings per week for games	next week Feb 3 + 5
Communication			
Spiritual wellness			
Dealing with crises and stress			

More about the
Family Strengths Research

The instrument for our initial research was a questionnaire having both open-ended and fixed alternative-type questions. The questions included were based upon what a review of the professional literature suggested might be related to family success or strength. Before the questions were submitted to families they were given to a panel of judges (family life experts holding a doctoral or master's degree in Human Development and Family Studies). The judges were asked to evaluate each of the questions in the instrument in the following ways: (a) is the question relevant to the topic being investigated, (b) is the question clear, and (c) do other questions need to be added? After the panel of judges had responded to the instrument, a pretest was administered to a small number of families.

The final form of the questionnaire (referred to as the Family Strengths Inventory) was then administered to the sample of 130 strong families in Oklahoma. Analysis of that data indicated that the six qualities which the strong families had in common were (a) expressed appreciation, (b) a lot of time spent together/things done together, (c) good communication patterns, (d) a high degree of religious orientation, (e) a high degree of commitment, and (f) the ability to deal with crises and stress in a positive manner. Later, this sample of strong families was compared to a sample of families that had experienced divorce within the past six months (these families were questioned, using the same instrument, about their relationships prior to the divorce) and to a sample of families experiencing severe relationship problems who were receiving counseling at state agencies. It was found that the divorced families and families experiencing severe relationship problems expressed to a highly significant degree far less of each of the six qualities (appreciation, time to spend together/doing things together, good communication, high degree of religious orientation, commitment, and ability to deal with crises in a positive manner) than did the strong families. In many cases the divorced families and families with severe relationship problems were completely lacking in any of these six qualities.

In the national and international studies that followed, we found that the strong families reflected the same qualities. We then shortened the questionnaire and used the shortened, revised Family Strengths Inventory in the last few national, international, and Nebraska studies we have completed.

In our statistical analysis of the revised Family Strengths Inventory, we have found each of the items (reflecting the six qualities) to be highly discriminating between those families with a high degree of family strength and those families with lower degrees of family strength. The instrument has been tested in many different studies with remarkably similar results.

THE SAMPLES

A total sample of 3,000 families contributed to the research upon which this book is based. All of the families were surveyed with a questionnaire. Ten percent of these 3,000 families were also interviewed.

The first 130 of these 3,000 strong families were from throughout the state of Oklahoma. In this study, Home Extension Agents were used as a resource for recommending strong families. We chose the Extension Agents because of their background training in family life, their concern for improving the quality of life for families, and their extensive personal contact with families in the community. Therefore, the criteria for being included in this first sample of strong families were (a) being recommended by the Home Extension Agent as being a strong family, (b) the family members themselves reporting a high degree of marriage happiness, and (c) the family members reporting a high degree of satisfaction with the parent-child relationship.

The remainder of the 3,000 strong families have participated in the various national and international studies which followed. Different methods were utilized for securing samples in these studies. In some of these studies the sample was obtained by running a news story in newspapers throughout the nation.

These samples of strong families included those who responded to the news story and who also rated themselves very high on marriage happiness and satisfaction with the parent-child relationship.

In other studies, such as the study of strong families in Germany, Austria, and Switzerland, the sample was obtained through a systematic random sampling technique. From a wide range of families with regard to family strength, those high-strength families were selected.

Most of the 3,000 families contributing to this research have been from the United States, with about 20 percent being from other countries (South America, South Africa, Iraq, Germany, Austria, and Switzerland). We have also studied Russian emigrant families in the United States. The U.S. families came from all regions of the nation. They represented all economic levels, all educational levels, many religious persuasions, both two-parent and single-parent families, and ranged in age from the early twenties to the mid-sixties.

We are continuing to study strong families. There is more to learn, so the Family Strengths Research Project continues to grow and is a major thrust for the Center for Family Strengths at the University of Nebraska.

Notes

CHAPTER 1

1. L. Harris, "Factors Considered Important in Life," *Louis Harris Survey Release*, January 1, 1981; G. Gallup, "What Americans Think about Their Lives and Families," *Families* (June 1982).

CHAPTER 2

1. We recommend that the reader take a look at the following books: W. H. Masters and V. Johnson in association with R. J. Levin, *The Pleasure Bond: A New Look at Sexuality and Commitment.* Boston: Little, Brown, 1974; W. H. Masters, V. E. Johnson, and R. C. Kolodny, *Human Sexuality.* Boston: Little, Brown, 1982.

2. N. Stinnett, J. Walters, and E. Kaye, *Relationships in Marriage and the Family.* New York: Macmillan, 1984.

CHAPTER 3

1. As quoted in N. Stinnett, "In Search of Strong Families," in N. Stinnett, B. Chesser, and J. DeFrain (eds.), *Building Family Strengths: Blueprints for Action.* Lincoln, Nebraska: University of Nebraska Press, 1979, pp. 23–30.

2. This quotation comes from *Joys and Sorrows: Reflections by Pablo Casals* as told to Albert E. Kahn. New York: Simon and Schuster, 1970, p. 295.

CHAPTER 4

1. A. L. McGinnis, *The Friendship Factor*. Minneapolis: Augsburg, 1979.
2. G. Bach and P. Wyden, *The Intimate Enemy*. New York: William Morrow, 1969.

CHAPTER 5

1. M. L. Jacobsen, *How to Keep Your Family Together and Still Have Fun*. Grand Rapids: Zondervan, 1969.
2. G. Rekers, *Spending Time Together*. Building Family Strengths Series. Manhattan, Kansas: Logos Research Institute, 1984.
3. This marriage would be termed a "vital" marriage in the parlance of John Cuber and Peggy Harroff. They divided marriages into five types as follows:

> *Conflict-habituated:* tension and ongoing conflict are the normal state in this type of marriage.
> *Devitalized:* this is the type that describes a great many marriages. The spouses start out full of love and eventually burn out. The relationship turns dull and humdrum.
> *Passive-congenial:* this type is very similar to the devitalized marriage except that these folks lacked excitement and interest from the start.
> *Vital:* spouses in this type of relationship share almost every part of their lives with interest and joy in each other.
> *Total:* this type of marriage is similar to the vital marriage except that spouses share even more of their lives. They often work together like the Sand Hills couple.

If you'd like to know more, see J. Cuber and P. Harroff, *The Significant Americans*. New York: Appleton-Century-Crofts, 1965.

CHAPTER 6

1. E. B. Williams (ed.), *The Scribner-Bantam English Dictionary*. New York: Bantam Books, 1979.
2. J. Lafferty, "A Credo for Wellness," *Health Education, 10* (1978), 10–11.
3. R. L. Banks, "Health and the Spiritual Dimension: The Relationship and Implications for Future Professional Programs." Unpublished doctoral dissertation, Ohio State University, 1979; K. N. Brigman, "Religion and Family Strengths: An Approach to Wellness," *Wellness Perspectives, 1* (1984), 3–9.

4. Archibald MacLeish is credited with this description of earth. A. MacLeish, "A Reflection: Riders on Earth Together," *New York Times,* December 25, 1968, p. 1.

5. From an exhibit in Muir's home, John Muir National Historic Site, Martinez, California.

CHAPTER 7

1. J. M. Lewis, *How's Your Family: A Guide to Identifying Your Family's Strengths and Weaknesses.* New York: Brunner-Mazel, 1979.

2. C. P. Gilmer, *Exercising for Fitness.* New York: Time-Life Books, 1981.

3. A. Kidd, "Dogs, Cats, and People," *Mills Quarterly,* (August, 1981), pp. 6-8.

4. T. H. Holmes and R. H. Rahe, "The Social Readjustment Rating Scale," *Journal of Psychosomatic Research, 11* (1967), 213–218.

CHAPTER 8

1. From a personal conversation with Dr. James Montgomery.

2. I. C. Kassorla, *Go for It: How to Win at Love, Work, and Play.* New York: Delacorte Press, 1984.

3. White House Conference on Families, *Listening to America's Families: Action for the 80's. A Summary of the Report to the President, Congress, and Families of the Nation.* Washington, D.C.: White House Conference on Families, November 1980.

4. L. J. Peter, *Peter's Quotations: Ideas for Our Time.* New York: Bantam Books, 1977.

5. J. Brothers, *What Every Woman Ought to Know about Love and Marriage.* New York: Simon & Schuster, 1984.

Bibliography

For more information about family strengths see the following sources. They are listed in chronological order, in each category, with the most recent first. This bibliography is a partial list of the publications, dissertations, and theses to come from this research.

BOOKS

Williams, R., Lindgren, H., Rowe, G., Van Zandt, S., and Stinnett, N. (eds.) (1985). *Family Strengths 6.* Lincoln, Nebraska: Department of Human Development and the Family, University of Nebraska.

Stinnett, N., Walters, J., and Kaye, E. (1984). *Relationships in Marriage and the Family* (2nd ed.). New York: Macmillan.

Rowe, G., Lindgren, H., Van Zandt, S., Williams, R., DeFrain, J., and Stinnett, N. (eds.) (1984). *Family Strengths 5.* Newton, Massachusetts: Educational Development Center.

Stinnett, N., DeFrain, J., King, K., Lindgren, H., Van Zandt, S., and Williams, R. (eds.) (1982). *Family Strengths 4.* Lincoln, Nebraska: University of Nebraska Press.

Stinnett, N., DeFrain, J., King, K., Knaub, P., and Rowe, G. (eds.) (1981). *Family Strengths 3: Roots of Well-Being.* Lincoln, Nebraska: University of Nebraska Press.

Stinnett, N., Chesser, B., DeFrain, J., and Knaub, P. (eds.) (1980). *Fam-*

BIBLIOGRAPHY

ily Strengths: Positive Models for Family Life. Lincoln, Nebraska: University of Nebraska Press.

Stinnett, N., Chesser, B., and DeFrain, J. (eds.) (1979). *Building Family Strengths: Blueprints for Action.* Lincoln, Nebraska: University of Nebraska Press.

PARTS OF OR CHAPTERS IN BOOKS

Stinnett, N. (1985). "Research on Strong Families." In G. A. Rekers (ed.), *National Leadership Forum on Strong Families.* Ventura, California: Regal Books.

Stinnett, N. (1983). "Strong Families: A Portrait." In D. Mace (ed.), *Prevention in Family Services: Approaches to Family Wellness.* Beverly Hills, California: Sage.

Lindgren, H., Stinnett, N., Van Zandt, S., and Rowe, G. (1982). "Strengths and Skills throughout the Life Cycle." In N. Stinnett, J. DeFrain, K. King, H. Lindgren, S. Van Zandt, and R. Williams (eds.), *Family Strengths 4.* Lincoln, Nebraska: University of Nebraska Press.

Stinnett, N., Sanders, G., and DeFrain, J. (1981). "Strong Families: A National Study." In N. Stinnett, J. DeFrain, K. King, P. Knaub, and G. Rowe (eds.), *Family Strengths 3: Roots of Well-Being.* Lincoln, Nebraska: University of Nebraska Press.

Stinnett, N. (1980). "Introduction." In N. Stinnett, B. Chesser, J. DeFrain, and P. Knaub (eds.), *Family Strengths: Positive Models for Family Life.* Lincoln, Nebraska: University of Nebraska Press.

Stinnett, N. (1979). "Introduction." In N. Stinnett, B. Chesser, and J. DeFrain (eds.), *Building Family Strengths: Blueprints for Action.* Lincoln, Nebraska: University of Nebraska Press.

Stinnett, N. (1979). "In Search of Strong Families." In N. Stinnett, B. Chesser, and J. DeFrain (eds.), *Building Family Strengths: Blueprints for Action.* Lincoln, Nebraska: University of Nebraska Press.

JOURNAL ARTICLES

Stinnett, N., Smith, R., Tucker, D., and Shell, D. (1985, Winter). "Executive Families: Strengths, Stresses and Loneliness." *Wellness Perspectives.*

Porter, R. W., Stinnett, N., Lee, P., Williams R., and Townley, K. (1985, Summer). "Strengths of Russian Emigrant Families." *Wellness Perspectives.*

Stinnett, N., Lynn, D., Kimmons, L., Fuenning, S., and Derrain, J. (1984). "Family Strengths and Personal Wellness." *Wellness Perspectives, 1,* 25–31.

BIBLIOGRAPHY

Knaub, P., Hanna, S., and Stinnett, N. (1984, Fall). "Strengths of Re-married Families." *Journal of Divorce, 7,* 41–55.

Casas, C., Stinnett, N., DeFrain, J., Williams R., and Lee, P. (1984). "Latin American Family Strengths." *Family Perspective, 18,* 11–17.

Stevenson, P., Lee, P., Stinnett, N., and DeFrain, J. (1983). "Family Commitment Mechanisms and Family Functionality." *Family Perspective, 17,* 175–180.

Stevenson, P., Stinnett, N., DeFrain, J., and Lee, P. (1982, Fall). "Family Commitment and Marital Need Satisfaction." *Family Perspective, 16,* 157–164.

Stinnett, N., Knorr, B., DeFrain, J., and Rowe, G. (1981). "How Strong Families Cope with Crises." *Family Perspective, 15,* 159–166.

Ammons, P., and Stinnett, N. (1980). "The Vital Marriage: A Closer Look." *Family Relations, 19,* 37–42.

Stinnett, N. (1979). "Strengthening Families." *Family Perspective, 13,* 3–9.

Stinnett, N., and Sauer, K. (1977). "Relationship Patterns among Strong Families." *Family Perspective, 11,* 3–11.

PERIODICALS

Milofsky, David, "What Makes Happy Families," *Redbook* (August 1981): 58–62.

Olds, Sally, "Do You Have What It Takes to Make a Good Marriage?" *Ladies Home Journal* (October 1980): 76, 78, 202, 204.

DISSERTATIONS AND THESES

Below is a list of works by our many graduate students who have contributed countless hours to the study of strong families.

Ammons, P. W. (1976). "Vital-Total Marital Relationships among Strong Families and Their Association with Selected Demographic and Personality Variables." Doctoral dissertation, Oklahoma State University, Stillwater.

Ball, L. L. (1976). "Communication Patterns in Strong Families." Master's thesis, Oklahoma State University, Stillwater.

Casas, C. (1979). "Relationship Patterns of Strong Families in Latin America." Master's thesis, University of Nebraska-Lincoln.

Collins, O. P. (1984). "Life Skills Development through 4-H: A Survey of Adolescent Attitudes." Master's thesis, University of Nebraska-Lincoln.

Elmen, J. (1981). "Sole Custody and Joint Custody: A Nationwide Assessment of Divorced Parents and Children." Master's thesis, University of Nebraska-Lincoln.

BIBLIOGRAPHY

Fricke, J. M. (1982). "Coping as Divorced Fathers and Mothers: A Nationwide Study of Sole, Joint, and Split Custody." Master's thesis, University of Nebraska-Lincoln.

Gutz, G. K. T. (1980). "Couples' Enrichment: Program Development, Implementation, and Evaluation." Master's thesis, University of Nebraska-Lincoln.

Johnson, S. (1984). "The Effects of Marriage Enrichment on Marital Adaptability, Cohesion, and Family Strengths." Doctoral dissertation, University of Nebraska-Lincoln.

King, J. (1980). "The Strengths of Black Families." Doctoral dissertation, University of Nebraska-Lincoln.

Leland, C. (1977). "The Relationship of Family Strengths to Personality Characteristics and Commitment." Doctoral dissertation, Oklahoma State University, Stillwater.

Luetchens, M. (1981). "An Analysis of Some Characteristics of Strong Families and the Effectiveness of Marriage and Family Life Education." Doctoral dissertation, University of Nebraska-Lincoln.

Lynn, W. D. (1983). "Leisure Activities in High-Strength, Middle-Strength, and Low-Strength Families." Doctoral dissertation, University of Nebraska-Lincoln.

Matthews, W. D. (1977). "Family Strengths, Commitment and Religious Orientation." Master's thesis, Oklahoma State University, Stillwater.

McCumber, A. K. (1977). "Patterns of Dealing with Conflict in Strong Families." Doctoral dissertation, Oklahoma State University, Stillwater.

Porter, R. W. (1981). "Family Strengths of Russian Emigrants." Master's thesis, University of Nebraska-Lincoln.

Rampey, T. S. (1983). "Religiosity, Purpose in Life, and Other Factors Related to Family Success: A National Study." Doctoral dissertation, University of Nebraska-Lincoln.

Sanders, G. F. (1979). "Family Strengths: A National Study." Master's thesis, University of Nebraska-Lincoln.

Sauer, K. H. (1976). "Relationship Patterns of Strong Families." Master's thesis, Oklahoma State University, Stillwater.

Smith, R. C. (1983). "The Family Life of Executives: A Descriptive Study." Master's thesis, University of Nebraska-Lincoln.

Stevenson, P. (1975). "Family Commitment: Application of a Theoretical Framework." Master's thesis, Oklahoma State University, Stillwater.

Stoll, B. (1984). "Family Strengths in Austria, Germany, and Switzerland." Master's thesis, University of Nebraska-Lincoln.

Strand, K. B. (1979). "Parent-Child Relationships among Strong Families." Master's thesis, University of Nebraska-Lincoln.

Tomlinson, D. L. (1977). "Power Structure of Strong Families." Master's thesis, Oklahoma State University, Stillwater.

Truitt, D. F. (1972). "Marital Need Satisfaction, Life Philosophies, and Personality Characteristics of Strong Families." Master's thesis, Oklahoma State University, Stillwater.

Wall, J. A. K. (1977). "Characteristics of Strong Families." Master's thesis, Oklahoma State University, Stillwater.

Weber, V. P. (1984). "The Strengths of Black Families in Soweto, Johannesburg, South Africa." Master's thesis, University of Nebraska-Lincoln.

Weber, W. C. (1981). "Families Cope with Stress: A Study of Family Strengths in Families Where a Spouse Has End-Stage Renal Disease." Doctoral dissertation, University of Nebraska-Lincoln.

Wright, R. M. (1975). "The Manner in Which Strong Families Participate in Activities Which Comprise a Large Segment of Potential Family Interaction Time." Master's thesis, Oklahoma State University, Stillwater.